FARMING ON THE EDGE

FARMING ON THE EDGE

Saving Family Farms in Marin County, California

JOHN HART

Photographs by Joan Rosen

UNIVERSITY OF CALIFORNIA PRESS   BERKELEY   LOS ANGELES   OXFORD

University of California Press
Berkeley and Los Angeles, California

University of California Press, Ltd.
Oxford, England

© 1991 by
The Regents of the University of California

Library of Congress Cataloging-in-Publication Data

Hart, John, 1948–
Farming on the edge: saving family farms in Marin
County, California / John Hart; photographs by
Joan Rosen.
    p.   cm.
Includes index.
ISBN 0-520-07055-0 (alk. paper)
—ISBN 0-520-07173-5 (pbk.: alk. paper)
1. Family farms—California—Marin County—Case
studies.   I. Title.
HD1476.U6M34   1991
333.76′ 17—dc20   90-36813
                                             CIP

Printed in the United States of America
9   8   7   6   5   4   3   2   1

CONTENTS

FOREWORD

Farming on the Edge tells the story of a diversity of people who have acted with good sense to define and protect their common interest. It is an interesting book, and it is a moving one because it gives hope.

Like many other people, I have grown used to thinking of our country as a battleground of competing interests, the future of which has seemed all too likely to be determined by "the forces of the marketplace." The supposed oppositions between country people and city people, country people and conservationists, conservationists and developers would continue to be resolved, I have feared, in terms of opposition, by force; and the country itself and most of its inhabitants would continue to be the losers.

This book suggests a possibility that is much different and much better. It suggests that opposition is not the truest way to define anyone's interest, and that some of our famous oppositions are more suppositional than not. It suggests that convergences and overlappings of interests can be identified, so as to enable diverse groups to cooperate to make local life better for everybody.

Over the past two decades, farmers, conservationists, government officials, and voters in Marin County, California, have learned to work together to preserve the farms, the farmland, and the farm people of the rural or "over the mountain" section of the county. The people of the urban eastern section wished to keep the rural western section from being covered with subdivisions. They wanted to preserve the "open space" of West Marin for the sake of all the needs that humans and other creatures have for open space. And they wanted to preserve themselves from the problems of traffic and congestion that would come with massive development "over the hill." It became evident that to preserve the open space they needed the farmers. And it became equally evident to the farmers that, to survive, they needed the sympathy, support, and help of the city people; they saw that, by themselves, they did not have the power to determine their own future.

The story of the changes of heart, of the cooperation and mutual help that followed these realizations will bring tears to your eyes if you are at all aware of the damages that have resulted from the competition of these "opposing interests." What the people of Marin County have accomplished is admittedly only a good beginning; their work is not complete and they will work amid difficulties for some time to come. But they have accomplished enough already to suggest what might be made possible everywhere by a clear perception of what local interests actually are and by the willingness to work together in good faith. They have shown us how the tensions among groups and interests may be dissolved in the spirit of community and how we can improve our places by improving our understanding.

In response to a variety of pressures, needs, and desires, and in ways inescapably halting, the many heroes of this book have changed their standards. They have learned to act in the interest of the community and of the land. They have begun the difficult, necessary recognition that these two interests are one.

If an outsider might be permitted a wish, I would wish that, as this Marin County conversation continues, it would involve more thought about the value of locally produced food. I am sorry that there has so far been no effort toward the local marketing of milk from local dairies (as there has been for other local food products). The securest guarantee of the long-term good health of both farmland and city is, I believe, locally produced food—that is, a local agricultural economy, with as little commercial intervention as possible between producer and consumer. Such an economy would make practical and economic connections between the people of the farms and the people of the city. These connections are necessary, and they imply further connections of mind and spirit.

Wendell Berry

ACKNOWLEDGMENTS

This project was conceived by Virginia Davis, Phyllis Faber, Joan Rosen, and Ellen Straus. Over a period of four years they interviewed and photographed more than fifty ranchers and other key players, contracted with this writer, and went through the vicissitudes of helping an idea grow into a book. For their trust, patience, and assistance, my thanks.

I am grateful to all the Marin County ranchers and public figures who gave their time to talk to us. Though only a fraction of these interviews could be featured in this book, each is somehow reflected in it.

Portions of the manuscript were reviewed by Bob Berner of the Marin Agricultural Land Trust; Matthew Guthrie of Forsher and Guthrie; Bill Kortum; Dewey Livingston, historian; Douglas Maloney, Marin County counsel; Larry Orman of Greenbelt Alliance; Marty Roberts of the Sonoma County Farmlands Group; and Paul Zucker, former Marin County planning director. All contributed valuable information as well.

I spent many hours in the offices of the *Point Reyes Light* newspaper in Point Reyes Station, reading several decades of local news coverage. Thanks to editor David V. Mitchell and staff. Similar thanks to staff at the Marin County Board of Supervisors for helping me track down elusive items from what already seems a distant past.

These people provided important information: David Anton of the California State Water Resources Control Board; former Marin County Planning Commissioners Margaret Azevedo and Hugh Dougherty; Keith Bartholemew of 1,000 Friends of Oregon; Rick Bennett, Sonoma County farm advisor; Don Brittsan, former Marin County farm advisor; Elton Brooks of the Milk Stabilization branch, California Department of Food and Agriculture;

Alan Bruce; James J. Dal Bon, Marin County assessor-recorder, and his staff; Geoffrey Geupel of Point Reyes Bird Observatory; Phyllis Hartley of the Marin County Farm Bureau; Jim Hope of Greenbelt Alliance; T. J. Kent, Jr.; Larry Kolb of the Bay Area Regional Water Quality Control Board; Fran Layton and E. Clement Shute, Jr., of Shute Mihaly and Weinberger, attorneys; former Marin County Supervisor Byron Leydecker; Paul Martin; Sherry Momeyer of the Milk and Dairy Foods Control branch, California Department of Food and Agriculture; Rixon J. Rafter; Mark Riesenfeld, Marin County planning director; Salem Rice, geologist; Jim Sayer of Greenbelt Alliance; John Siebert of the California Cooperative Creamery; Will Shafroth, Western regional director of the American Farmland Trust; Sol Silver, former Marin County Advance Planning chief; Robert Tancreto of the North Coast Regional Water Quality Control Board; Karin Urquhart of the Marin Conservation League; and Carol Wittmeyer of the Sonoma County Planning Department.

Thanks also to Sue Abbott, Ray Ahearn, Richard Bolman of the Sonoma County Department of Environmental Health, Dwight Caswell of the Sonoma County Farmlands Group, Dan Deevy, Peggy Lauer, Mark Manion, Julie Manson, Bill McCall, Mike Moore of the Petaluma Planning Department, Tim O'Hara, Rich Peterson, Richard Plant, Angela Poppe, Ray Rinaldo.

I am indebted to Anthony R. McClimans for an insight about the de facto political parties in Marin County during the 1960s.

At several points I have built on language originally drafted for the report, *The Search for Permanence: Farmland Conservation in Marin County, California,* published in 1982 by People for Open Space (now Greenbelt Alliance), to whom my thanks.

John Hart

I thank Ellen Straus for guiding me around West Marin to meet all the wonderful people who appear in this book. It was a privilege and a joy to glimpse their world. I also thank Steve Bobzien for his ready assistance in printing the photographs and Meg Quigley for the loan of an extra enlarger and lens.

Joan Rosen

A rancher remembers:
Philip Respini of Marshall.

Prologue ■ THE EXPERIMENT

A hillside above Tomales Bay, and the California fog moves in. Not much gets in its way: a rock outcrop, a barn, a row of pale-barked eucalyptus trees. Cattle, somewhere, are lowing. The bay—as long for its width as a Norwegian fjord, a saltwater river marking the line of an earthquake fault—glimmers across to a darker, forested shore.

There was a time when government planners looked forward to forty-three thousand acres of suburbs on this waterside. "By 1990," a Marin County official said in 1971, "Tomales Bay will probably look like Malibu." That it doesn't look like Malibu—how it came about that it doesn't look like Malibu—is a story of much more than local interest.

It's not some inaccessible backwater, this bay Tomales. It lies just outside a major metropolitan area, forty miles and a bridge away from San Francisco, within reach of six million people. The urban part of Marin County, across a couple of chains of hills, has the highest per capita income in the state. Even out here, the price of land per acre is well above what might be justified by the narrow profits of dairying or the erratic returns of cattle ranching and sheep raising—the main agricultural pursuits. Land speculators have bought and sold here; city-sized developments have been proposed.

We know in America what to expect when matters reach such a point. There may be regret; there may be protest; there may even be ordinances passed. But once development pressure begins seriously to be felt, one thing leads to another, an avalanche of change. Sooner or later the countryside is gone, "converted," as the jargon puts it, made part of the urban scene.

Here that process was well begun. Then came a quiet revolution: something almost resembling a palace conspiracy of able planners. An election. A crucial one-vote shift on a county government board. A jerky turnabout in policy. After 1971 urban growth, in western Marin County, was officially out of favor; continued ranching was in.

But the fact that the policy shifted is not really the story. Such re-beginnings have been attempted in various places; in the typical county or town, the new rules never really take or gradually lapse as public attention fades. The remarkable thing about what Marin County did is that, in the years since 1971, it has kept on doing it: that West Marin was actually drawn back, like a piece of wood already blackening, from the urban fire.

This success was achieved in two overlapping stages. The first was the period of coercion. Having imposed restrictive zoning against strong opposition, the county flatly maintained it: no exceptions, no weaseling redefinitions, no compromises. To be blunt about it, urban people imposed their will on unhappy and outnumbered rural ones.

So stage one. Stage two was a far stranger development: the building of an alliance, by some called unholy, between the regulated and the regulators. Promoting this convergence were certain of the county's conservation leaders, who helped to focus what now amounts to a social contract: forswear development out west, and the urban east will do what it can to help your agricultural business prosper—or at least try to refrain from getting unnecessarily in the way.

It's too early to call the Marin experiment, simply, a success. A lot of farmers, especially dairy farmers, still worry about the future. Land prices are still climbing, bid up by urban refugees with copious money to spend. The pressure for massive development, now in abeyance, could quickly rise again. An agricultural land trust, established to protect farm use forever through sophisticated "development rights" transactions, is just beginning to show results.

But incomplete as it is, the Marin County effort is already a recognized model, one of the patterns that are studied wherever people get together to work on preserving farmland in their own regions. If rural areas near cities anywhere are to survive on a large scale, it is likely to be on some such terms as these.

Tomales Bay

One ▪ WAITING FOR THE END

The county of Marin, San Francisco's richest suburb, has recently been worth an easy laugh: has been, at least since Cyra McFadden wrote her funny, deadly *Serial,* a symbol of self-conscious trendiness. But for a much longer time than that—for a century, in fact—this same small region has been famous on quite other grounds: as a beautiful piece of the planet, forest and farm and headland; and for the extraordinary things done here, against all odds, toward keeping that beauty whole.

Going back even a bit farther, the county has had yet another kind of fame: as an agricultural leader, the premier dairy county in California. Marin will never again outmilk all rivals, as it did as late as 1900, but its recent work on farmland protection makes it once again a notable farm county.

The Laboratory

The place with all these reputations is a wedge of land between waters: the Pacific Ocean on the west and, on the east, San Francisco Bay and its various intruding baylets. The southernmost promontory is nose to nose with San Francisco at the Golden Gate. Behind these coastlines spreads a little Appalachia of hills, part grassy, part brushy, partly in woods and forest. A wandering central divide splits the county into an accessible bayside strip and a larger, more rugged seacoast portion. The passes between are not high, but the roads that cross them are, even today, two-laned and wandering; in the old days they were terrible.

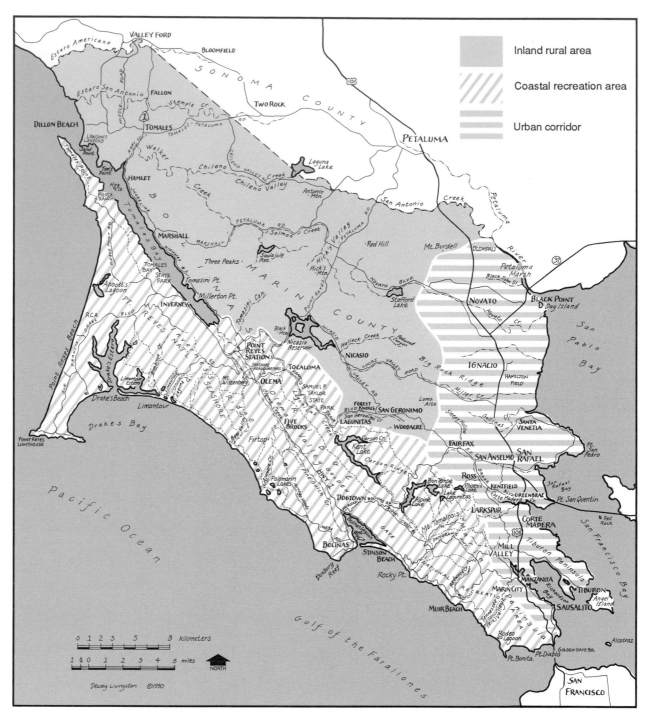

Legend

- Inland rural area
- Coastal recreation area
- Urban corridor

Marin County, California. Cartography by Dewey Livingston.

Except for a few valley floors, there is little room in this hilly triangle for traditional large-scale agriculture. What the county does possess is some of the state's best natural rangeland. The abundant grass, the cool summers near the shore, the unusually long green season in spring—all gave the early dairy farmers a natural edge over competitors north, south, and inland. And the customers—the largest urban population in the state—were right next door.

When the dairy trade was at its height, the western part of the county was the busier side. At various times in the 1800s, West Marin villages—Nicasio, Olema, Tomales—campaigned to replace the eastside mission town of San Rafael as county seat. But East Marin, facing San Francisco Bay and the cities spotted around it, presently began to pull ahead in population. In 1937, when the Golden Gate Bridge attached Marin to San Francisco, the eastern county was knitted into the emerging regional metropolis; West Marin, for the moment, remained outside the urban world.

After World War II, few expected that isolation to last. The waves of development that were sweeping around the bay would presently leap the hills. Everyone knew that; it only wanted a few roads.

In the 1950s, as the state highway planners sketched the outlines of the future freeway system, they had big ideas for West Marin. Route One, the tortuous coastal highway, was to grow into a four-lane "parkway," and completely new freeways would punch through the hills from San Rafael and Novato in the urban zone to Point Reyes Station, informal capital of the West Marin farm belt. A county planning study listed other possible corridors and concluded zestfully that "major traffic facilities" would someday have to be built in all of them.

Plainly, if even a portion of this new asphalt was laid, access would no longer be a barrier to urban growth in West Marin.

Nor did it appear that West Marin farmers would be especially well equipped to hold out against development pressure. By midcentury, the agricultural advantages of the region seemed gone. With transportation easy and fuel prices low, closeness to market was no longer so important. Big dairy farms in the Central Valley, feedlot operations sustained by subsidized federal water, looked awfully efficient compared with the small homegrown operations in Marin. And as the ranches "over the hill" in East Marin sold out one

In Chileno Valley

Holstein herd in Chileno Valley

by one, to be replaced by suburban neighborhoods—as formerly struggling farmers walked away with the proceeds of their last and most lucrative harvest, the land itself—there seemed little reason for a landowner to worry much about, or invest much time and money in, the *agricultural* future.

And so it became the fashion—even among ranchers? especially among ranchers—to question whether the industry was viable, to anticipate the arrival of Cashout Day. Though many families, deeply attached to the land, had no intention of selling and indeed turned down what seemed, by the old rural standards, to be generous offers, there remained the sense of an approaching end.

That end seemed only to move closer in 1959, when the federal government announced its plan to buy some fifty thousand acres of the coastline for a park.

Point Reyes National Seashore

In the late 1950s, federal park planners were searching the coasts of America for primitive seashore areas to set aside for the public, especially near cities. Of the shockingly few candidates they found, the most impressive was Marin's Point Reyes Peninsula.

Point Reyes is a big, triangular flap of land sewn on, as it seems, to the western shore of the county, a peninsula on the peninsula. It's an odd and separate country, part wild, part pastoral, always a little mysterious; a land of conifer forest and fog and sea-lion coves, and again of open, lupine-blazing fields. Big dairy ranches covered much of it. Now the Park Service wanted all of it. After a bitter controversy—the landowning families, many on the point for generations, were not happy to be so targeted—Point Reyes National Seashore was authorized in 1962.

The park was of course a victory for conservationists. In national terms, it was a prototype for a whole new species of national parks near cities. Locally, it ensured that at least a part of West Marin would remain generally as it was. It changed the way people thought about the region. (The familiar backyard hills, a national treasure!) Without the National Seashore, later preservation efforts might not have been possible at all. But from an agricultural point of view, the park meant the end of isolation, the beginning of what seemed uncontrollable change.

As visitors poured out to the newly accessible beaches, woods, and headlands, it was plainly time to do some very specific thinking about the future of the rest of West Marin. That thinking took the forms conventional for the time. The Marin County Board of Supervisors asked the state Division of Highways to get moving on the proposed freeway from San Rafael in the urban belt across the hills to Point Reyes Station, now at the park's front door. The state highway planners obediently got started on the task, difficult in this tangled topography, of choosing a detailed route.

Meanwhile, the supervisors set planners of their own at work on a first blueprint for the development of the countryside adjacent to the new park.

Limantour Beach, Point Reyes National Seashore

An uncertain future

"To Finish Us Off"

It isn't easy, today, to put hands on the glossy document that resulted from this work. One of the few copies now in existence of the West Marin General Plan is tacked up in a dairy barn, the one belonging to rancher Al Poncia.

Poncia first saw the plan in 1966 in Point Reyes Station, at a public hearing at the West Marin School (an unimposing complex where the major issues affecting the region always seem to get argued out). He was a relative young-ster then, preparing himself to take over management of the family dairy ten miles up the coast near Tomales town. As a soon-to-be rancher interested in cows, not condominiums, he didn't like what he saw. "They were setting it up," he remembers, "to finish us off."

They were indeed. Up and down the Olema Valley south of Point Reyes Station; up the gently sloping, windy hillsides east of Tomales Bay; on up to the Sonoma County line, the West Marin plan proposed to put a population of some 125,000 people. Outside the green expanse of the National Seashore, the master plan map bristled with colors. Residential expanses, shades of yellow and brown. Shopping centers, red. One large commercial freckle lay on the diked-off tidelands at Point Reyes Station. In its final form, the plan showed 43,000 acres of urban land at an overall density of 1.15 units to the acre.

Of several possible objections to this plan, one jumped out at you. The area under study closely matched the path cut across Marin by the San Andreas Fault, source of the great earthquake of 1906. (People still living in West Marin remember: the sky to the south turned red as San Francisco burned.) Now tens of thousands of people were to live within a mile or two of the fault. Worst of all, near Point Reyes Station, a major shopping center was planned right on top of the fault and on bay muds covered with fill—the shakiest possible kind of ground.

Didn't the planners of the day consider these dangers? They did, a little; they put a mild warning in the final document. But in the end they saw no alternative to full-scale development. We forget what it was to be in the planning trade in those days, when the pressure to develop land seemed a force as natural, ubiquitous, and unopposable as gravity. Local government in California in the 1960s had so little practical ability to set land use that any plan that didn't simply echo current trends was hard to carry out. During this period, the whole West Marin region could, in theory, have been cut up into 7,500-square-feet lots (about six to the acre).

County Counsel Douglas Maloney put it this way: "Some schlock merchant can come in and butcher up the land and put in a bunch of junk, and there is probably little the government can do to prevent this."

And where was the county's large and influential corps of conservationists? In fact they worked very hard on the West Marin plan, but all their energy

This essay, written when the author was in the fourth grade at one-room Lincoln School in Hick's Valley, won a prize from the county on the occasion of National Agriculture Week, 1986.

I will tell you how milk is produced. First you have to get your cows into the barn then you pull down a lever so the cows can come into their stalls. Next you have a little hose by each cow and you wash her udder off. Then you put the machine on the cow to get the milk out. So they don't kick, you turn a knob then feed comes out for the cows to eat. If you have automatic takeoffs, the machine will come off by itself.

That means that all milk has gone into the tank that holds thousands of gallons of milk. When the cows are outside, you have to feed them. Some people have tractors and some have computerized barns. That means that when each cow goes into the barn the computer reads the cow's ear tag number and so many pounds of feed come out of the feeder. Each night a milk truck comes to the barn and takes the milk to the creamery. They run it through the processor and bring it to the stores. Some day I would like a dairy farm of my own.

went into a fight to keep the supervisors from raising the density—slightly. The preliminary version had foreseen a density of 0.88 units per acre; three out of five supervisors favored, and eventually imposed, the figure of 1.15. In retrospect, the difference between a little less and a little more than one dwelling per acre seems like no difference at all; at the time, all sides thought it was crucial.

Attention was diverted, too, to trouble on Point Reyes. With less than half of the National Seashore land acquired, the Park Service had run out of money. One of the ranches within its prospective boundaries was being sold off in expensive pieces; a splendid headland farm at the far northern tip had passed into the hands of a speculative holding company called Land Investors Research. Time was running out. Public opinion rallied to save the park. Zones and land-use plans, after all, are shifty, unreliable, complex, and evanescent things; a park is theoretically forever.

So West Marin, bay and beach and wood and pasture, seemed about to be torn apart. If the park advocates succeeded, some parts would actually become wilder. If the planners and highway engineers pursued their courses, vast sections would eventually turn urban. Few—it appeared as late as 1970—could remain anything like what they were: ranch country, cow country, a rugged gray-green hinterland. Of the many things that might be done with the land, the one that no one seemed to speak for was the use being made of it already: the production of milk, meat, and wool.

Ralph Grossi, a former Marin dairyman who now runs the American Farmland Trust, remembers how it was. "Everybody was talking about how many houses their ranch would accommodate and where in the state they were going to go to buy their next dairy," he says. "You sort of got to sitting on the front porch with your suitcases packed."

Al Poncia didn't feel that way, but he knew plenty who did. At the meeting where he got his first look at the West Marin plan, he felt almost alone in his dislike of it. "There were many, many people there," he recalls. "And all of the ones who were the spokesmen of agriculture were basically saying, Marin County agriculture is dead, and that's it. . . . They believed the whole county would develop. They may actually have wanted it to."

"I'll Tell You What I Want": Al Poncia (Tomales)

Al Poncia steps over to his kitchen window, looks down across slanting pasturelands to the gentle valley of Stemple Creek, and warms up to his favorite subject: grass.

Poncia knows grass. He knows it in the scientific sense—the bladed stuff, the real thing, the *Gramineae*—and he knows it in the looser casual sense: all those short green plants that make up a meadow, things that cows can eat, clovers and vetches and weeds and even thistles. Thistles he could talk about for hours. "If you overgraze, it seems like you get them. If you don't graze enough, damned if you don't still get them, too." (But the cows will eat them, if you cut them tender and mix them with other cuttings in windrows.)

That a dairyman should ponder these things is not as automatic as it might seem. In many parts of the country—in California's Central Valley, for example—operators rarely think about grass, the green stuff sticking from the ground. They think about *feed,* of course—it's their biggest single expense— but feed is something that arrives from elsewhere. Sometimes from very far elsewhere. And the cows themselves, milling around on hardened earth or concrete pads or even in huge buildings where they stay most of their lives, may never crunch a stem that is still attached to the soil.

That's drylot ranching: large scale, undeniably efficient by some measures, patently industrial. Some think it's the shape of the future, the sleek new model against which Marin's much smaller, family-run hill farms can't possibly compete. If Marin can in fact compete (it looks as if maybe it can), it's partly because of the grass.

We don't think of it that way, or even stop to notice, but western Marin County, with adjacent parts of Sonoma, is California's greatest native pasture.

Al Poncia, dairyman, Tomales. "The place is more important than what you can get out of it. I want us to be here for a long, long time."

Go inland, and the climate gets hotter, the grass correspondingly sparser (except of course in irrigated fields). Go north along the coast, and the forests close in. Go south, and the grassland gives way to indigestible chaparral. Here, just here, are the really extensive grasslands of the coastal belt, where the maritime climate, cooled by summer fog, prolongs the season of green.

That's why, in the days before feed could be cheaply moved from region to region or grown on irrigated desert soils, the North Bay counties were so natural a dairy center. The local cattle, fewer in number then, lived all year long on locally raised feed (straight from the pasture or as stored silage). Today the picture has changed; fodder for today's much larger herds is mostly imported, and the once telling advantage of the local climate has dwindled.

Yet not to zero. Ask Al Poncia. He finds that his cattle can live off the yield of his green hillsides ("There's no better grassland in Marin") for a quarter of the year, sometimes as much as a third, cutting tens of thousands of dollars off his annual feed bill. "It's my equalizer with the valley," says Poncia. "That's why I keep referring back to grass."

Keeping that grass at its best takes work. He is carrying out an elaborate seeding and treatment plan, drawn up for him by a consultant, to make his good land better. After experiments with straight chemicals, he's back to manure for fertilizer (along with all the nitrogen his clover roots are fixing in the soil). Recently he bought an aeration tool, a machine like a jawful of drill bits, that breaks up soil to let air in. (Compaction, the packing down of soil so that water doesn't pass and roots have trouble pushing through, is one of a farmer's less notorious problems.)

A lot of grass has pushed up on these hills since 1972, when Poncia scandalized his Farm Bureau colleagues by speaking up in favor of strict agricultural zoning. Now he'll admit to being, at times, a little tired.

"This must be one of the most demanding jobs in the world," he says. It was always muddy, strenuous, and a little dangerous ("Sooner or later, you are going to get hurt"). Now it is nonstop as well. When he was growing up, he looked forward to the slack time in the middle of the day, between morning and evening milkings. The family might drive down to Blake's Landing on Tomales Bay: demolish a picnic lunch, lie on the little beach, hitch up an outboard to go waterskiing past Hog Island. That made up, partly, for the lack of real vacations. But with the sophistication of the dairy business today—the narrowing profit edge, the always greater pressure to produce, the continual tricky decisions—the odd bits of leisure are few. Life, like compacted soil, loses its little open spaces.

A couple of years ago it all started getting to Al. There was a bad patch economically. He got a nasty cut on his forehead shoving a cow into a squeeze chute. He was chagrined to discover that he had allergies ("I was supposed to be the tough little Italian"). Allergies, even, to *grass*. Depression settled over him like one of those unrelenting summer fogs ("they're better for cows than for people"). He began to talk to his wife, Cathie, about getting out of the business, even moving away. "You're not supposed to admit these things if you're a rancher," he says. "You people 'over the hill' relate to these problems more.

"This place has been what I've loved on the one hand, but I've been its prisoner on the other."

The love, though, has proved to be stronger. Whatever the Poncias ultimately decide about staying in the dairy business, staying on the ranch appears to be a given.

"I've got four kids and I'll tell you what I want to happen here. I want the ranch to stay intact and have a place for the young people to come even if they don't actually ranch it. I'm probably an idealist and a traditionalist and a sentimentalist fool.

"When I die, I want some of my ashes to go up on the hill over there.

"What could be better than to be plowed into the earth and be born again with every season's new grass?"

On Government Soil: The McClures of Point Reyes

When the Park Service descended on Point Reyes at the end of the 1950s, it was not welcome there. One rancher told a congressional committee, "We have fought hard to make our end of the point what it is today. And, gentlemen, we are going to fight hard to keep it."

That fight was lost—and won. The park came; but within it Congress outlined a "pastoral zone" where ranchers could remain on the land. At first this was regarded (in some quarters) as a temporary concession. Then came the revival of interest in Marin agriculture, and the recognition that—if the agricultural belt was to survive at all—the Point Reyes portion of it could not very well be dispensed with.

Point Reyes, after all, had been the heartland, the first and famous dairy district, with the foggiest fog, the greenest grass, the most hospitable terrain. Even today, 20 percent of Marin's milk is produced on the point. And some of the largest and most modern operations in the region flourish under the federal landlord.

Three generations of McClures: Bob,
Ron, and Jim (left to right). "We don't
look the same with our hats off."

None more than the McClure ranch far out on Pierce Point Road, where Jim, Ron, and Bob McClure—father, son, and grandson—manage one of the county's premier dairies.

The original James McClure arrived from Ireland in 1890 at the age of eighteen. Then, too, there was a major landlord: the almost imperial Shafter-Howard family, which owned most of the peninsula and rented it out to carefully chosen tenants in ranches labeled with alphabetical names. The McClures' first place was "G," at the head of Drake's Estero. Schooners came into the estuary then; James eventually acquired an interest in the vessel *Point Reyes,* which took butter, cheese, and hogs to San Francisco from landings all over northwestern Marin. Son Jim remembers cutting butter into cubes and stamping each with the ranch's individual mark.

The McClure ranch of today is not "G" but the old "I" ranch, inland from Abbott's Lagoon. The site is a sloping plain, screened from the sea by low hills and by the summer fog that closes in, often for weeks at a time.

Jim McClure (son of the first James and like him a tenant) came to "I" in 1930. In 1939, the Shafter ranches in the area were finally offered for sale to their occupants. Jim was the first to close a deal. With all the energy of new ownership, he set out to build a model dairy herd. By 1950, his Jerseys were ranked third in the state. He won't say how he did it: "Just luck, I guess."

When you drive up to the McClure ranch, the first thing you notice is the plowed fields that extend on both sides of the road. More than most Marin properties, the place looks like a *farm.* On few other dairies do terrain and water supply permit such lavish planting: almost a square mile of oats and vetch, harvested for silage.

Jim's son, Ron, was six when the family moved to "I" ranch. He remembers milking by hand; he remembers trips to Inverness when the jaunt was a muddy adventure. It was partly to get a better road that another McClure made a gift to the county of spectacular little McClure's Beach, a National Seashore attraction today. "In those days," Ron recalls wistfully, "there were seven dairies on this road." Now there are three.

Then came the park, and the McClures found themselves once again on land they did not own. Ron wishes that the federal government had contented itself with buying the immediate shoreline—"It's the beach that people want"—and had left the interior ranches alone. Still, matters haven't turned out badly. They get along well with the park, and when the family's original "reservation of use" expires, they can reasonably expect to remain.

The future didn't always look so promising. At one point the Park Service proposed to offer ranchers only five-year "use permits"—too short to allow long-term planning, too tenuous to encourage investment, not enough time for paying off a loan. But the ranchers' allies in government and in the conservation movement took up the issue. The result appears to be an acceptable deal: the ranchers will get what amount to long-term leases, but in signing them they will also commit themselves to meet certain explicit standards for grazing pressure and erosion control.

Ranchers used to worry that park visitors would spook the cows. It hasn't worked out that way. Ron tells his tourist stories with amusement, not annoyance. "If there was a cow calving by the road, man, the people would stop, the cars . . . once in a while someone would come to the door and say, 'There's a cow having a calf, I think she's having trouble.' And I'd say, 'Okay, I'll be right there.' Well, I'd just have to take my time and hope she'd had it by the time I got there. Boy, the audience; man, the people!"

The park is not an issue for young Bob McClure; he's lived with it all his life and hopes to do so for decades more. He knew from the start that he wanted to stay on the ranch, on this ranch, and prepared himself systematically, studying the dairy business at California Polytechnic State University in San Luis Obispo. He's been home and working here full-time since 1983. Still in his twenties, he is young to be co-manager—one of the new generation that is keeping West Marin dairying vital.

In the late 1970s, when energy prices spiked, the cost of importing feed from the Central Valley began to hurt. It was then that the McClures made the decision to put their best land under the plow for silage. (The change did raise some eyebrows among park-watching conservationists.) Since then, the ranch has been the county's one example of a full-scale feedlot dairy. These cows don't wander around the landscape, grazing; their food, all of it, comes to them.

The silage raised on the ranch doesn't replace imported feed, though it knocks a significant 25 percent off that massive bill. Alfalfa (not grown in the fog belt) is still essential. "Cows do better if they get ten pounds of it a day," says Bob. The McClure feed barn is a regular supermarket: stacks of alfalfa at either end and, between them, bins full of soybean meal, sugar-beet pulp, whole cottonseed, and hominy. Outside sits a feed mixer, mounted on a truck, spinning augers protruding from the side. Depending on commodity prices and much else, the feed mix changes frequently. A nutritionist with a computer calls the shots.

So the McClures, innovative from the start, keep going. Recently they rearranged the stalls in the milking barn to the very efficient configuration called a double-ten herringbone. One worker can milk their 360 cows in five hours. (When you have a herd that large, you do time-and-motion studies.) Like all dairy operators, they are constantly working to upgrade their animals. Their milk yield averages 7.8 gallons per day per cow—they are shooting for 8 gallons even. With milk price supports dropping and competition sharpening, "You've just got to get more efficient," Ron says. "All the time."

La Padrona: Sharon Bianchini Doughty
(Point Reyes Station)

La Padrona, the hired hands call her. The boss, feminine gender. It's a title of some distinction, for Sharon Doughty is a rarity among dairy proprietors: a woman in sole control. Since the death of her former husband, dairyman Bill Bianchini, she's been running the family's 780-acre block of land on Tomales Bay a couple of miles north of Point Reyes Station and doing, thank you, quite well.

Many women work, and work hard, on dairies. Why so few women managing them? The urban mind suspects stereotyping, mere social habit. One writer, oblivious to the lurking pun, has suggested replacing the term "dairy-*man*" with the gender-neutral "dairi*er*." Such views get little backing in the countryside. Even in these mechanized days, it's generally felt, a manager has to be ready to do a lot of plain grunt work—the sort of work where muscle mass still matters. "If the help left," says lightly built Doughty, "Bill could go out and buck hay or whatever, and I'm not going to do that." She insists: "It's not a woman's profession."

But her experience also shows that it's possible to separate the management from the purely physical work and make a no-nonsense success of it.

Sharon Doughty, born a Mendoza, grew up on a ranch out toward the tip of Point Reyes. She attended a one-room school on the point (founded by her grandfather at his own expense): twelve students in eight grades. One thing she didn't learn was the Portuguese her parents occasionally spoke at home, mostly for matters they wanted to keep private from the kids: "What a waste!" She does speak Spanish, as any rancher just about has to, these days.

She went on to get a B.A. in accounting from the University of the Pacific. But when she looked for work, she found jobs scarce for women with that skill. Her response was to add another: she went back to school for a teaching credential and taught junior high in Petaluma for several years. Her flair for numbers became known, however, and she wound up as something of a circuit-riding accountant, doing books for a number of ranches (including her father's) and for a creamery or two. Nightly homework could run to four hours.

Sharon Doughty runs a dairy outside Point Reyes Station.

*Sharon and her daughter, Kathleen
Bianchini, queen of the Portuguese Holy
Ghost Festival, Sausalito*

Along the way she got to know quite a bit about the complexities of the dairy business. But actually running a dairy was the last thing on her mind.

In 1969, as the West Marin General Plan was promising an end to agriculture, she married dairyman Bill Bianchini. They had a ranch near Two Rock on the Sonoma County line for several years, then moved to the present spread, a sleek wedge of land sloping down from a gentle ridge line to the bird-haunted shallows at the head of Tomales Bay.

Then, in the spring of 1984, Bill died. Among the things Sharon wrestled with that year, while a brother-in-law pitched in to keep the operation afloat, was the decision: sell out or take over?

Common sense said, sell out. It wasn't a case of losing an ancestral home. She had marketable, if undervalued, skills. She also had two daughters, then ten and thirteen, to finish raising.

What pulled the other way? More than anything else, it was the community—the people around her, related or not, who came forward with their support. Neighbors offered to help out. The longtime hired hands, Pablo and Antonio Lopez, urged her to continue. So, importantly, did her daughters. "And my father kept saying, 'Of *course* you can do it.'"

Early in 1985, she decided to give it a try.

At first, the hours were horrendous, the list of things to learn, unending.

But the community was there, enfolding. Family. Friends. Neighbor Bobby Giacomini. Veterinarian Bob Fisher, who spent "hours at that kitchen table" briefing her on problems, procedures, medications. And, says Doughty, "I was amazed at how much I actually knew." She had picked up a lot of know-how working with her father; she had picked up more than she thought possible from Bill. "Things he talked about, I remembered."

"I started to manage the ranch in February. By June, I thought I'd live. By December, I knew I loved it." And she threw a party for the many who had helped.

She regards herself even now as learning, feeling her way. "I don't do anything fancy here. Dairying is a very complicated business. You can make or lose a lot of money." But she is proud of ranch statistics: she's boosted average milk production from 16,000 pounds per animal per year to 18,600. She no longer gets up at three in the morning to make sure the milking goes right, but she still spends a lot of time in her shipshape corner office in the barn. "Accounting! Organization!" An extension phone hangs there and beside it a list of important numbers. "It's probably the only milking barn in the county," she says with a laugh, "that has the hairdresser's number on the wall."

For half an hour every afternoon she sits on a fence and watches the cows come in. She checks for animals in heat and also for any that are limping, acting weak, or showing signs of the malignant condition called cancer-eye. Spotting animals in trouble is a skill that takes some learning. Her top hand, Pablo, still amazes her: "There's no one like him for *seeing*. For looking at a cow and saying, 'I think there's something wrong with her' . . . there's an instinct about it."

In 1987, she married Steve Doughty, a dredging supervisor turned private investigator. The herd remains her job. "I love taking a ride to the top of the hills and checking things over and looking out across Tomales Bay." Like most Marin ranchers, she sets great store by her green pastures. "The cows are healthier when they're out on the grass. There's less disease." The pastures on the lower edge of the ranch, next to the coastal highway, are among the best around. Sometimes they stay lush for half the year.

"No question about it," says La Padrona, using the proprietor's first-person plural, "we do have good front fields."

Two ■ BACK FROM THE EDGE

Al Poncia, worried about the ranching future, got involved in the Marin County Farm Bureau. As any volunteer knows, that sort of thing is a slippery slope: unless you get awfully good at saying No, you run the risk of being put in charge. And so it was that, early in 1969, just as the West Marin General Plan became official policy, Poncia was chosen to be Farm Bureau president— not as the result of a campaign, certainly not because of his offbeat ideas, but because he was conscientious and available.

However unplanned, his arrival in the post was strategic. He got there just in time to see the whole sky change: to witness and even discreetly to help along a transformation, almost shocking in its suddenness, of public policy and official thinking.

The Roots of Change

Early in 1969, the Marin County Board of Supervisors had affirmed a plan calling for major, widespread development in West Marin. By mid-1971, the board was carrying out a plan that called for an utterly different future—the western county as a mixture of ranches, parks, and widely separated villages. How could it happen? How could it happen so fast?

As is often the case with apparently rapid change, the transformation was less abrupt than it seemed: it had in fact been taking shape for years, just under the surface of business as usual, unrecognized.

Throughout the 1960s, there were, in Marin's allegedly nonpartisan local politics, two distinct parties or blocks. These two factions were not Republi-

Rural self-sufficiency

can and Democrat; they were pro-planning and anti-planning, for and against some management of growth. As the decade passed, the public grew more and more anxious to see development held within limits and open space protected. And yet—perhaps because the real parties were not recognized—that support did not translate into a majority on the five-member board of supervisors. Time after time, on issue after issue, the planning advocates found themselves on the losing end of votes of three to two.

For a moment in the middle of the decade, however—in 1965 and 1966—the pro-planning party commanded the board. It used that opportunity fully. The three like-minded supervisors, Peter Behr, Byron Leydecker, and Tom Storer, eased out the planning director of the day, a man whose ideas they liked well enough but whose ability to execute seemed lacking. In his place they recruited, from Brookline, Massachusetts, a brash and efficient youngster named Paul Zucker. The board majority gave Zucker a free hand and encouraged him to develop something the county had never had before: a countywide plan, one looking at all Marin, cities and countryside, as the single organism it so obviously was.

During 1966 Zucker set the effort going. He hired a completely new set of top assistants. He got the supervisors' approval on a detailed, multiyear work program. And he started to push the idea of a joint city–county planning council to supervise the long-range planning work. (Since each incorporated city in California is its own land-use authority, larger-scale planning, county-wide or regional, can be done only by special arrangement.)

At the core of the planning work was a transportation study, a look at the whole question of movement in Marin: the roads, the traffic expected from planned developments, the transit service present and to come. Putting it all together, what kind of sense did the pattern make?

The study showed very quickly that it made no sense at all. As an eventual report would dryly put it, "existing plans project too much development to be served by too little transportation." Nobody had taken a critical look, until then, at all the urban expansion the county and its various independent city governments had in mind; nobody had figured out in detail what roads, built and maintained at what expense, it would really take to serve the new communities. Now they knew. Highway 101, the single major north-south route along the bay, would have to become a monster, a double-barreled New Jersey turnpike of a road; at the Golden Gate, there would have to be at least one additional bridge; feeder freeways would snake through every valley—all enormously destructive, in this hill-packed, erodible country, and quite possibly too much to pay for.

In laying out their notions of "inevitable" growth, one valley at a time, the complaisant planners of the past had been steering into an absurd, an unworkable future.

The urbanization of West Marin, then taken for granted, was part of that impractical future—indeed the least workable part of it. New neighborhoods and new freeways west of the hills, pouring their commuters into the 101 corridor, would have multiplied congestion; by spreading suburbs to its farthest shore, the county would have lost forever the chance to channel growth in corridors where transit service has a fighting chance to function well.

Plainly, for the sake of the rest of the county, the coastal belt should have a relatively uncrowded future.

Front porch at the Jensen ranch, Tomales

But before the planners had progressed very far toward these conclusions, an election once again shifted the balance on the Board of Supervisors. In 1967, the free-market or let-'er-rip philosophy was once again in control. The West Marin plan (sketched out before Zucker's arrival) was stripped of some good features it had possessed in draft, adopted, and then amended to permit still more building. In 1969, guided by the plan and ignoring the safety warnings of geologists, the supervisors approved a 340-unit condominium development on eroding bluffs near the village of Dillon Beach at the mouth of Tomales Bay.

Planning Underground

Yet during this whole expansionist period, the planning engine started up in 1966 kept right on running, thanks partly to the quiet work of County Administrator Alan Bruce; in his role as budget writer, he steered money toward the planners and away from road improvements into West Marin. It helped that the federal government picked up much of the tab through planning grants. Then, too, the planners were now reporting not only to the supervisors but also to the successfully established City–County Planning Council; this fact may have insulated their work to a degree.

But the most significant shield was probably this: the planners' labor was simply not taken seriously in the quarters where it might have been seen as a threat. As planner Sol Silver recalls, "advance planning wasn't part of the real world. They were willing to let us play." Alan Bruce agrees: "It was easy to give lip service to the planning work. It wasn't dangerous."

The general public, during these years, seems to have known very little about what was going on behind the scenes. The rethinking was after all a job in progress, ideas changing from month to month, outlines scaffolded in jargon and routine. The press missed the story entirely. But all the while public opinion was swinging farther against the old development ideas. People were unsure just what it might be possible to substitute; but they knew they didn't want suburbs shore to shore. State laws meanwhile were beginning to change,

History

offering local government more land-use regulation tools. Resisting these powerful currents, though, was a board majority that liked the old idea of the future just fine.

In 1970, Paul Zucker made an unfortunate career move. He ran against one of his supervisor bosses in the fall election, lost, and was shortly out of a job. But the same election brought victory to the informal planning party. Arnold Baptiste of Novato was elected to replace retiring Supervisor Bill Gnoss. Gnoss, a well-liked moderate and a swing vote on many issues, had nonetheless come down consistently in favor of maximum development in West Marin; Baptiste joined Michael Wornum and Peter Arrigoni in a new majority opposed to such development and ready to back newfangled planning ideas.

The Revolution of 1971–1972

What followed, as idea and political will combined, seemed to take even the participants by surprise. It wasn't merely that a different viewpoint now had the upper hand: as time went on, the terms of the whole discussion shifted.

The radical notions of one month became the commonplaces of the next. Especially after the public became involved, things moved very rapidly indeed (the press often lagging painfully behind).

A well-timed nudge came from the state. Back in 1965, in a first rather feeble effort toward farmland preservation, the legislature had passed a law encouraging each county to establish "agricultural preserves." Within each area so designated, property tax breaks were made available to farmers who agreed to keep their land in agriculture for a certain period. (Agreement took the form of a contract with the county, good for ten years, and automatically extended each year if neither side canceled. Lost tax revenue was replaced by the state.) Marin had designated such a preserve (the first county in the state to do so), and ranchers here and there had signed contracts.

By 1970 the legislature had strengthened the law. It required now that the land in "agricultural preserves" be limited to uses that were "not incompatible" with agriculture. That meant, in effect, farm zoning. Marin had to look at the future of its farmland with new seriousness.

For counsel, the supervisors turned to the ranchers themselves, appointing six to a temporary Agricultural Land Conservation Advisory Board. The list reads like an honor roll of old West Marin names: Grossi and Giacomini, Tomasini and Stewart, Marshall and Silveira. There was one outsider: Harold E. Gregg, ebullient executive director of the Marin Conservation League. It is tempting to believe that Gregg argued against the recommendation finally made: namely, to sidestep the state challenge. The "agricultural preserve" should be redefined to include only the scattered properties actually under contract; only those properties needed to be zoned; and the future of the rest of West Marin should be considered later.

The county planning staff protested that farm zoning applied at random here and there was pointless. The Planning Commission labeled the solution "short, easy, and unsatisfactory." But the supervisors at first agreed to follow the ranchers' lead: they decided "in principle" to cut back the preserve. Fortunately, they took no formal action.

In June 1971, the larger planning story broke; a first version of the new countywide plan appeared. The county planners—still under the flag of the

BACK FROM THE EDGE   33

Merv McDonald, cattle rancher near Marshall

City—County Planning Council—took it before the public in a series of meetings and further publicized it in a tabloid, *User's Guide.*

What struck you immediately about the new Marin Countywide Plan was the sharp distinction it drew between eastern and western Marin: the eastern corridor marked for continued growth; the land west of the divide reserved for agriculture and for recreation. "The plan for two kinds of Marin," a local paper headlined, and that was indeed the essence of the thing. Technically, though, the plan divided the county into three corridors: the eastern urban strip; a central region of ranches (and watershed land); and a coastal band with mixed uses, containing parkland, farmland, and here and there a cluster of resort development.

Citizens' reaction to the new scheme was one-sided: an almost incredulous recognition and relief, criticism only of detail. The new plan was essentially

Peter Dolcini counseling a Mexican farm worker's child in Spanish

simple; it was clearly presented; and—most of all—there seemed hope that much of it could actually be carried out. Driven now by public opinion, the process moved with astonishing speed.

In August, the supervisors repealed the two-year-old West Marin General Plan ("the most cockeyed plan ever devised," County Counsel Douglas Maloney told a West Marin citizens' group. "Nobody likes it").

In September, the supervisors acknowledged what was now obvious: they had made a misstep in agreeing to shrink the agricultural preserve. They confirmed it within its old broad boundaries. Agricultural zoning would have to be applied to the bulk of West Marin.

What form should it take? The planning staff and Planning Commission were already kicking the question around. The bright new technique of the day, just coming into use in several California counties, was control of parcel

One-room school in Hick's Valley

size. In this approach, the regulators do not insist directly on farm use or uses compatible with farming. Rather, they order that lots cannot be split below specified sizes. The theory is that such restriction will more or less automatically preserve agricultural use.

By 1971, several counties had set very large lot sizes, even as high as one thousand acres. But these zones applied mainly to low-value grazing lands, dry, steep, remote, and out of the probable path of urbanization. Marin was trying something harder: to divert a current already flowing, some thought irrevocably, toward urban growth.

Using the parcel-size approach, what size should Marin set? Clearly, for the needs of local ranching, pieces under a hundred acres were not very useful.

And yet the supervisors feared that too large a minimum size could be challenged successfully in court as too great an intrusion on property rights. The planners came up with a range of options. In the end, it was the county's lawyer, Maloney, who determined the balance point: sixty acres, he advised, was as high as the supervisors could safely go.

A-60

In January 1972, hearings on the new parcel-size zoning began. They got exciting when star witness William W. Wood, an agricultural economist with the University of California at Riverside, came to town. At first he was a guest of the Farm Bureau, and many people (not acquainted with the leanings of the bureau's president, Al Poncia) expected him to speak against the zoning.

Wood duly began by doubting that agriculture was viable in Marin over the long term. It should be treated as an interim use, maintained for the sake of overall planning goals. But how long was "interim"? "It might be anywhere from one to one hundred years."

"You may still have the option of preserving these lands," Wood told the Planning Commission. "Whether it is still politically feasible is the question at hand. . . . I don't know the relative political pressures that are brought to bear or can be brought to bear in this county."

What density zoning did Wood recommend? Because of the conflicts that arise when urban people settle among farms, "I suggest to you that almost a zero density is about the only compatible one." He strongly hinted that a zone of two hundred acres would seem reasonable to him. Suddenly, A-60 looked moderate. The next time he testified, Wood's way was paid by the county.

At the end of February, the rezoning of West Marin got underway. Where the old general plan had allowed at least 51,000 units and the de facto zoning many times that number, the new rules would permit, at most, 3,200 new lots and dwellings in all the region (outside the sixteen existing villages). The new zone was labeled A-60: *A* for agriculture, 60 because most properties could not be divided into parcels smaller than sixty acres, with, on each such parcel, just one house allowed. (In areas where parcels were already smaller, less stringent rules applied.)

So complete a reversal had bitter opponents. Most prominent was the Marin Property Owners Association (MPO), which made a stand at every bend in the winding road of policy change. The regulation, MPO members protested, would lower property values, force housing prices up, wipe out the retirement income of ranchers. Key argument: by restricting development to this degree, the county was trying to secure at no cost the open space it should be buying. "It's unfair," said Richard Nave of MPO, "to ask people who own land to preserve it for us without paying for it." A San Anselmo man complained, "Where will it all stop? I am convinced that the planners, backed by the conservationists, mean to separate us from our land." The association promised to sue.

Both opponents and supporters of the new plan seemed willing to speak on the ranchers' behalf. The supporters offered the hope that zoning would "save dairying." The development side scoffed. "I don't see," said Richard Nave, "how your staff can look at dairying in Marin and say they are protecting a viable industry. These ranchers are just eking out a living."

And the ranchers—for whom so many seemed to be speaking—what did they think about the change? No mystery about that: they hated it. As a group, they followed the Marin Property Owners' line almost, if not quite, all the way. Ranchers traditionally had an absolute view of property rights and a distaste for government and all its works. And sincere though they were in their love for the land, many ranchers were accustomed by now to the thought of cashing in on it. Like landowners anywhere when prices are rising, they were, in some corner of their minds, speculators.

It is easy to forget, looking backward from a friendlier time, the bitterness of that A-60 battle.

Despite this, not all ranchers opposed the new rules. Only a pair of known mavericks—William and Ellen Straus of Marshall, outspoken conservationists for years—openly endorsed them; but there were also a few essentially conservative ranchers, mostly young, who saw A-60 as a tool in their fight to stay on the land. It was highly significant that one of these was Farm Bureau President Al Poncia. He couldn't persuade the bureau to stay neutral—the board did vote to oppose A-60—and he once had to back down after venturing a favorable comment on his own. Nevertheless, the bureau under Poncia

Beef cattle ranch

made no attempt to rally its members *against* A-60. This reticence, where a loud call to arms might have been expected, said much.

"Some people plan," futurist Alvin Toffler once remarked to a United States Senate committee. "Others are planned upon." In 1972, the ranchers of Marin were, perhaps unavoidably, among the planned upon.

Room with a view

All through 1972, in a dozen or so hearings, the rezoning process continued. As it became clear that minds on the board would not change, the arguments grew more perfunctory. In the November election, the West Marin supervisorial seat was open. One candidate criticized the new policies, suggesting that ranchers should be paid for speculative value lost. The other, Gary Giacomini, made support of A-60 the theme of his campaign. Giacomini got the seat. The pro-zoning majority stood at four to one. The threatened lawsuits were not filed.

And within months of the rezoning, three ranches north of Marshall on Tomales Bay—several thousand acres that had been in speculators' hands—were sold once more to ranchers, at prices that the ranchers could afford. However bitter to some, the A-60 medicine seemed to be having an effect.

Reinforcements

The battle—the initial battle, anyway—was decided. Then the cavalry came. Its arrival still mattered.

For planning and environmental action, the beginning of the 1970s was the liveliest period we have seen. Laws, elections, court decisions, vast new parks: the world seemed to be changing day by day. Though few *local* governments changed their attitudes as rapidly as did Marin's, much was happening at higher levels. And the county's brash steps in land-use regulation were reinforced quickly and strongly by acts of Congress and of the statewide electorate.

On October 28, 1972, President Richard Nixon signed a bill creating the 34,000-acre Golden Gate National Recreation Area. This new federal park took in a swathe of coastland between Point Reyes National Seashore and the Golden Gate, creating a unified publicly owned greenbelt that is still unmatched in the nation. The new park boundaries took in the green Olema Valley south of Point Reyes Station—the most gently pastoral of West Marin landscapes and the one most vulnerable to pressures of development.

Still more significant was the action California's voters took in the November 1972 election. Frustrated by the way local governments were fumbling away the beauty and accessibility of California's thousand-mile coastline, the electorate set up a new Coastal Commission and six regional subcommissions to administer coastal planning. The new bureaucracy had final say over land use in a coastal strip half a mile wide; it also had the unambiguous mandate to protect coastal resources, agriculture among them. In many counties, this new regime forced a drastic change of course. Marin had already set its new direction, but the state rules underlined and reinforced the change.

During the three-year life of the original California Coastal Commission, they brought one notable modification in the structure of the Marin Countywide Plan. As first enacted, the plan called for new clusters of tourist-serving development in West Marin, especially along the eastern shore of Tomales Bay. County planners thought that such enterprises would be compatible with agriculture; conservationists doubted it; ranchers, whatever their thoughts about compatibility, mostly supported such development. After jarring controversy, the county approved a large shoreline lodge north of Marshall. But the Coastal Commission would have none of it. Since 1975, when this decision became final, the thought of resort development outside the existing villages has been dead.

That, however, is getting ahead of the story.

PROFILES

In at the Beginning: Peter Behr (Inverness)

Nobody has had more to do with the way western Marin County looks today than Peter Behr, former city council member, planning commissioner, supervisor, state senator, and presently a sort of conservationist—elder statesman-at-large, respected, it appears, by all sides and all tendencies.

Behr, who says "planning was never my main interest," started his career in the early 1950s as a planning commissioner for the city of Mill Valley. He soon moved on to the city council, where he had a freeway to fight.

In the late 1950s the state was pushing to replace Marin's winding coastal highway, Route One, with a multilane expressway. First stretch to be worked over: the rugged passage from the outskirts of Mill Valley over the hills and along the cliffs to Stinson Beach. "They weren't going to bother with bridges," Behr recalls. "They were just going to take all the dirt and throw it in the canyons." But citizens' opposition was not so easily disposed of. At a preliminary public meeting with state staff, "we packed a gymnasium. They had long charts and we had long charts. We beat them back there." Then the highway commission itself came and held a hearing. "That time we stopped it dead. They got so discouraged after seven hours of complaints they said they wouldn't come back. Whereupon there was an enormous cheer.

"But they always do come back," he cautions, "to these long-range plans. They never forgive and they never forget. Overexpansion of these roads is a risk even today."

Behr went on to the Board of Supervisors in a throw-the-rascals-out recall election that displaced a ruling coalition known as the "Courthouse Gang." His arrival had an immediate solid result for the landscape of West Marin: with his vote, the board now narrowly endorsed a full-sized Point Reyes Na-

42

Peter Behr and Phyllis Faber (in hat), listening at Family Farm Day.

tional Seashore. Without that decision, the park plan would have shrunk from fifty-three thousand acres to twenty thousand.

It was Behr too, who, turning to his friend, Congressman Clem Miller, secured an unusual grant of federal funds to prepare a detailed land-use plan for the territory bordering the National Seashore. Express purpose: "having it not be the usual kind of junkyard you go through before you get to a national park." Mary Summers, a highly respected former county planning director, was hired to do the work. But Behr was shocked at the result, the bustling West Marin General Plan: "Those plans were scary . . . the total population projected was beyond anything that anyone thought possible."

If Behr had continued to have two like-minded colleagues on the board, the West Marin General Plan might well have been dumped in 1967 instead of 1971. But the 1966 election put his viewpoint in the minority. The plan was not only accepted but amended to a higher density.

Of the various things that Behr and his allies accomplished before they lost control, two stand out. First was another holding action against a freeway, this time the proposed multilane road from San Rafael to Point Reyes Station. By the end of 1966, this Route 17 freeway, though technically still planned, was stalled for good. The second key act was the hiring of Paul Zucker, with instructions to produce a Marin countywide plan. "He sort of took us by storm." In 1969, after Behr left the board, Zucker, accused of tactlessness in dealing with developers, was nearly fired; Behr came before his former colleagues to plead against the move. By the time Zucker did lose his job, a year later, the new plan had a life of its own.

Meanwhile Point Reyes National Seashore was in trouble again: acquisition money had run out and the Nixon administration declined to spend more, even if funds were appropriated. Behr was a leader in the dramatic Save Our Seashore campaign that finally salvaged the park. That was one of the very first times, he notes, that ranchers and conservationists found themselves on the same side.

Did Behr, as supervisor, have a clear idea that all West Marin, not just the park, could remain rural—and not just relatively rural but absolutely so: agricultural, open, to the casual eye unchanged? "No, I didn't. We didn't know it was possible. . . . I do think the environmentalists had an affection for agriculture that was more implicit than explicit. It became explicit later."

And the future? Behr does not rule out the possibility of big developments in West Marin. "If some major developer came in and went to work on the board, I'm not so sure. . . . Projects reach a certain size, they have a life of their own." Development might also be forced from above. From time to time there is talk in the legislature of imposing urbanization on certain rural areas, regardless of local plans, as a sort of blind stab at solving housing problems.

"But," he adds, "I don't actually think we're going to see any significant change unless the dairy industry goes broke. And the dairy industry is not going to go broke. They have the most powerful lobby of any industry in the country."

After his stint on the Board of Supervisors, Behr went on to Sacramento for two terms as a state senator (among other accomplishments, he authored the state's Wild Rivers law). In 1978 he decided he'd had enough of the political life, but he keeps his hand in on local issues: at this writing, he's chairing an advisory committee on the future of Tomales Bay.

It is Point Reyes National Seashore that remains his first affection. He and his wife, Sally, have a home within five minutes' walk of the park boundary, up in the Bishop pines and huckleberries at Inverness. In recent years, he's watched the great park get wilder. "The tule elk are back. They're planning to bring the bald eagles back. And before I die, I hope to see the wild turkey restored to the National Seashore."

Beef from the Greenbelt: JoAnn Stewart (Olema)

The auto accident wasn't her fault and the other driver's insurance company paid. When she got back on her feet, young JoAnn Stewart of Olema took the hard-earned windfall and went shopping. She bought thirty Hereford heifers and started her first beef cattle herd.

She was twenty-two then, just out of college, and already clear about what she meant to do. "Even as a little kid in grammar school," she remembers, "I wanted to be a rancher. (I'm never as happy as when I'm with my cows.) And I wanted to be in this valley."

One day in 1958 that hope was shaken. She was out riding, up on Mount Tamalpais, with a friend. "And he said, 'Did you see this morning's paper? They're going to take your area for a park.' And I said, 'They can't do that.'" She laughs. "How wrong I was."

Point Reyes National Seashore would secure for permanent public use one of the last great empty spaces near San Francisco. It would open up miles of wild beaches and thousands of acres of dusky virgin forest. It would also give the government title to a dozen or more big dairies, including much of the Stewart ranch at Five Brooks south of Olema, and the Stewarts' hundred-year-old home.

"Believe me, I didn't like it," says JoAnn. "I didn't like having our land taken away. I didn't want my world to change."

She got an argument, though, where she least expected it: at home, from her father, Boyd. Boyd Stewart quietly favored the park. Saw in it the one real

The Stewart Ranch and Breeding Farm, Olema

alternative to subdivision. Believed that, in the end, the ranchers who sold would be able to stay on the land. "We used to have some real battles in this house," JoAnn recalls.

The park came. Slowly. The original legislation had not allowed enough money. By the end of the 1960s the ranchers, assured that they would receive both good prices for the land and the right to remain there if they chose, were themselves asking Congress to appropriate the needed funds.

Even before the project was complete, a campaign was under way to build a second vast preserve alongside it. When this new Golden Gate National Recreation Area had been assembled, you could walk or ride horseback from the foot of the Golden Gate Bridge to the farthest peninsulas of Point Reyes without ever seeing a Private: No Trespassing sign. The companion park took in those parts of the Olema Valley that Point Reyes Seashore had missed—including the remainder of the Stewart ranch.

This time JoAnn didn't mind. "They had me broke in by that time. And it's worked out fine; we get along with the park very well." Boyd Stewart is more lyric. "One valley they won't subdivide is the Olema Valley, ever. One

JoAnn Stewart, Black Angus breeder,
with her horse. "There have been horses
in the Stewart family for a long time."

cemetery they won't move so they can put houses on it is the Olema cemetery. . . . I'd make a very poor socialist, but wouldn't it have been a shame if this park hadn't gotten here?"

Now the Stewarts and their cows are tenants, resident on an official national treasure. They seem to enjoy the special responsibilities this gives them. They graze few animals and take exemplary care to leave the range in good condition. They also select their stock for gentleness. Any cow in the herd that shows signs of being "upheaded"—aggressive toward people—goes immediately to slaughter.

Some years ago JoAnn discontinued the dairy business. She now raises Black Angus cattle for beef. "I have a cow-calf operation. That means that I have the mother cows, breed them, calve them out, raise the calves to be eight or nine months of age, and sell them to the feedlot for finishing; in the meantime, I've put the cow back with the bull and she produces a calf every year."

That describes any beef operation, but Stewart meant hers to be special. She was determined to raise heavy, high-quality animals without the questionable aids that much of the industry relies on—gimmicks like hormone-releasing implants and low-level antibiotic dosing in food. "I just wouldn't use those methods," she says.

But where was the feedlot that would use the same care while it raised her animals to final weight? Close by, as it happened. Down the road in Bolinas, Bill Niman and Orville Schell were just going into the business, guided by ideas much like JoAnn's own. (Schell, a noted author, would soon take on the mainstream livestock industry in an exposé entitled *Modern Meat*.) The Stewart ranch became the feedlot's first and principal supplier. Niman-Schell beef is of the gourmet class that undergoes blind tastings, like quality wine. "Bill Niman is conscientious in the grains he buys and the hay he buys. And he buys good healthy vigorous animals. Like mine."

Producing a better beef animal is also a matter of genetics. "We have a long-term breeding program, selecting the right bulls, selecting replacement heifers, and culling those animals that are aggressive. The bloodlines of each animal are traced back to their great-grandmothers and grandfathers."

Unlike the dairy rancher, whose product enters an ocean of milk, JoAnn can watch her crop from start to finish. "I'm able to see my cows alive in the feedlot; I'm able to see them hanging on the rail. I go to North Bay Breakers (the place in Santa Rosa where the animals are actually cut into the different cuts of meat). And then—I have done this, the whole way through—I go down to Living Foods in San Anselmo. I don't wear ranch clothes. I don't let anybody know who I am. I just sort of browse around the butcher shop and look at the meat in the case and listen to what people say. I know that that's my meat. It delights me."

There's a nice accord between Stewart's drive for quality and the special demands of ranching in a park. "It works together. The better care you take of the land, the bigger your calves will be. If you take good care of your cows, you're taking good care of your pasture, too." Again, the gentler animals, the ones least likely to get into trouble with park visitors, turn out to yield superior meat as well.

"I think we put out a West Marin product that is number one," says JoAnn Stewart. "And I begin it."

"We're Going Our Way": Ed Pozzi (Tomales)

The hardest thing Edward Innocente Pozzi ever had to do was to get on a bus in Petaluma to go away to war, leaving his aging parents to milk ninety-five dairy cows the old, slow way: by hand; alone.

Some ranch kids don't know for a long time whether or not they want to stay with the land. Pozzi, an only child, always knew. But in 1945 Uncle Sam, in the form of the Petaluma draft board, brushed aside arguments of hardship and sent him to the Pacific. Parting from his parents then caused him more grief than did their deaths years later. "I still cry about it," he says. He very nearly does now.

This fierce loyalty—to family, to the land, to a way of life—is what strikes you most about Ed Pozzi.

His family came over piecemeal from 1880 onward, part of the great wave of Italian immigrants. Following a common pattern, a couple of youngsters—grandfather Charlie, aged fifteen, and his brother, Louie—made the trip first, scouted the territory, and went home for others. "After that, they always came with somebody who'd been here before." Following another common pattern, they began as employees and very soon worked up to owning ranches.

The family went through some good times and bought land. They got through the Great Depression by "half-starvation and good luck" and emerged with more land than before. By midcentury the expanding clan had half a dozen properties in northwestern Marin and western Sonoma. "We could have had half of Marin County for forty or fifty dollars an acre. But we always believed in operating on our own money."

Away in the Marines, Pozzi was proud of his physical strength. "An officer asked, 'How did you learn to walk so good?' I said, 'I walked behind a plow, sir.' He said, 'I thought so.' But I was worth more as a farm boy than playing around with those guys."

Ed got back from the Far East in 1947 and soon received a coming-home present: the Lawlor ranch in the far northwestern corner of Marin, his home ever since. He married Regina McCarthy, of a Modesto ranching family. They were to have nine children.

For many years the Pozzis operated a dairy; in 1978, he switched to white-faced sheep, along with the beef cattle he'd been running all along. (The two species are complementary grazers, favoring different plants, so that the two together can be more profitable than either alone.) "I think the dairy business has done itself in," says Pozzi, "being too big and too much hired labor and hauling everything in . . . this country where we are is all going to be for grazing sheep and some cattle."

Coastal California lamb has a better flavor, Pozzi feels, than the New Zealand import or domestic lamb from the Central Valley, "a different taste—it's like Italian French bread." Then there's wool. "Nothing replaces wool." That the United States is a net wool importer strikes him as ridiculous.

He admits that sheep are not long on brains: "They'll lie down in such a way that they can't get up. They're so stupid they'll die."

An optimist about his own enterprise, Pozzi is worried by what he sees happening around him. A glance at the real-estate section, with its speculation-boosted prices for rural land, alarms him. He warns that ranchers who get overextended buying such land will regret it. He's grieved when he sees farms being split up after a death or removed from production for lack of an

"No For Sale signs on this ranch." Ed Pozzi.

interested heir. Unusual among West Marin landowners, he finds the existing sixty-acre zoning far too lenient: "I don't know why Marin County stays with it. They should put it up to one house to three hundred acres, as far as I'm concerned."

Where he sits in the far corner of the county, Pozzi is almost surrounded by 3,700 acres that are vacant, "bankrupt and so on." The empty land makes him itch. "When nobody lives on it, everything goes to hell." Tenant farming is just as bad. He is musing on buying some of that ground for his sons.

Pozzi lost his wife to cancer in 1985. But the family goes on. All three of his male offspring are now at home and ready to keep the tradition going. "There won't be no For Sale signs on *this* ranch. . . . My nine, we talk about it lots of times. Buyers come. No, we're not interested, we say. We're a farm family. We're going our way."

Three ▪ CRISIS AND ALLIANCE

By the end of 1972 the new direction for West Marin was firmly established—on paper. Reality was a good deal shakier. In the parts of the region that were not parkland or under Coastal Commission permit authority, county policies alone stood against development pressure; and there was reason to wonder whether they would do the job.

The thought was not so much that the county might change its mind (though that seemed possible). Rather the concern was that, despite the new policies, agriculture in Marin would continue its long decline and, as it drifted toward extinction, would take with it the legal justification of the policies themselves.

A-60 was (and is) a regulation with two purposes, interlocking but not identical. Its first function was a negative one: it prevented massive development outside the eastern urban corridor. Its second purpose was positive: it supported agriculture by protecting it against competing uses of land. Especially at the beginning, the open-space meaning was the one that people mostly thought about; but it was state farmland-protection law that had opened the door to A-60, and the protection of agriculture was the primary stated purpose of the zone. How long could such a policy be defended if the dairies continued to fail?

In a more general way, too, the presence of agriculture shielded A-60 from legal challenge. Though government's power to set land use was broad and getting broader, it was (and is) not unlimited. Zoning need not permit the *most* profitable use of land, but it ordinarily must permit *some* profitable use. A viable dairy industry meets that test. Take that industry away, and the chances of a successful legal challenge to A-60 would increase mightily.

"I hope," candidate Giacomini had said about A-60, "that this zoning will save dairying." He might equally well have put the hope the other way around: that dairying would save the zone—and with it the whole structure of the countywide plan.

Uncertain Health

In 1950, there had been some two hundred dairies in Marin County; in 1960, one hundred fifty. In 1972, there were fewer than one hundred. Discernible in the not too distant future was the problem of "critical mass." To survive, an agricultural industry needs to have a certain number of participants, a certain acreage, a certain amount of product. If it falls below these thresholds, it will no longer be able to support the complex network of services on which it in turn depends. Providers of many types—for instance feed suppliers, livestock veterinarians, credit establishments, creameries—all need to maintain a certain volume of business. As the number of customers drops, some suppliers go out of business and competition lessens. Monopolies appear and prices rise. If the shrinkage continues, services start to disappear altogether.

One rancher describes neatly how it works. "There are several feed mills in Petaluma. I try to remain loyal to one supplier, but every now and then I check to see what the other guys are doing. My supplier knows that, because I tell him. 'Well, listen, you're $2.00 higher,' I'll say. 'That's only fifty bucks on a twenty-five-ton load, so I'll let it pass this time.' He gets the message. You tell me what grain prices will do when there's only one feed mill in town."

Nobody knows just what the critical mass of Marin and Sonoma counties' dairies is. (The two make up a single dairy belt). In 1972, the system was plainly still large enough to be efficient. But how much further shrinkage could the belt endure?

Nor were the remaining West Marin dairies in reassuringly good condition. The years of uncertainty had had their cost. Ranchers aware of the possibility of development—whether they looked forward to it or feared it—had hesitated to sink money into the incessant maintenance and occasional expensive innovation that their industry requires. Statewide, dairies of the day were

Boyd Stewart, National Seashore partner

getting 14,500 pounds of milk per cow per year; Marin dairies, a 1973 county study found, were getting 13,300. In the Central Valley, a worker could milk forty to seventy cows in an hour; in Marin operations, the average was thirty-three cows an hour. And Marin ranchers were notably older, on average, than their competitors statewide. Marin, once the state's leading dairy county, had fallen far behind.

A-60 zoning, grudgingly accepted for the time being, had not put an end to the doubt. Mixed signals from the county did not help. On the one hand, the authorities used agriculture to justify A-60 zoning and fortify the urban-rural split; on the other, they seemed to regard this justification as an expedient, a stopgap. While A-60 rezoning was going on, and for several years after, there was official talk of A-60 as a "holding zone," something to do with the land until better and presumably different plans could be made. The amount

Valley Gothic

actually said about agriculture in the countywide plan and its surrounding documents was disconcertingly small.

These things gave the farm community the idea that it was being used: that, to the planners and conservationists "over the hill," agriculture was merely a means to an end, a grubby necessity almost, some way to justify holding the land open. Behind the talk of saving ranches, ranchers could almost smell the thought, "It can't *all* be parks." In these suspicions they were largely correct. Real respect for the ranchers, real regard for their loyalty to the land, real appreciation of their difficult way of life: these were to come. At the moment of policy change, they were rare.

Land prices both reflected these doubts and nourished them. It was estimated that a typical acre of Marin County hillside was worth $150 to an agricultural owner. But land was actually selling, in some areas, at $1,000 an acre—a very high freight (in those days) for thin-soiled land without irrigation water. Fortunately, since the typical Marin ranch had been in one family for generations, few youngsters actually had to buy property from profit-minded strangers. Yet high land prices did make it hard for an expanding operation to secure more land. One expectation during the A-60 battle—the fear of one side and the hope of the other—was that the zoning would cause prices to drop toward purely agricultural values. In a few cases, this happened, but in general the effect was only to slow a continuing rise.

Starting to Talk

Once it became clear that A-60 was for real—that it was not going to be rolled back any time soon—a few people on either side of the issue began, shyly, tentatively, to search for common ground.

There were various channels, various starting points. Supervisor Giacomini recalls going to a Farm Bureau meeting—"It was like I had a horrible disease." But, he recalls, he did succeed in arranging a meeting between Farm Bureau officials and Jerry Friedman, then chairman of the Environmental Action Committee of West Marin, soon to be Giacomini's new appointee to the Planning Commission. Out of such conversations grew a body called the Rural Forum, whose membership list included, besides the Farm Bureau and the Environmental Action Committee, the Marin Conservation League, the Coast Chamber of Commerce, and the Marin Property Owners Association. Ignoring the many points on which they could not agree, the participants soon found a number on which they could. The forum was the first of several successive organizations that, over the years, have bridged the interest groups.

About this time, the Farm Bureau established a Dairy Waste Committee to study pollution problems and invited non-ranching interests to join; Harold Gregg of the Marin Conservation League, never one to accept that ranchers and conservationists were natural opponents, appointed as league representative a man who was both: dairyman William Straus of Marshall.

The supervisors, for their part, set up an advisory group of ranchers and promised to consult it before acting on farm issues. The county also hired a study on the viability of agriculture and what might be needed to ensure it. (The results, seven months later, boiled down to a big If: agriculture in Marin could work, if the zoning remained in place and other policies lined up in its support.)

These steps were real, but tentative and small. They cost little, and they did not do much to ease the resentment that still prevailed on the ranches—the sense of being abused, as by a colonial power, by people "over the hill."

"Off the Camel's Back"

Then came a blow from another direction, one that seemed to the ranchers to bear out their most cynical fears.

In 1973, after years of talk, the California State Water Resources Control Board got serious about controlling water pollution from dairies. Cows make a lot of manure. Compared with urban sewage, barnyard runoff may be ten times as "rich," ten times as charged with those organic compounds that are, depending on where they wind up, either valuable fertilizers or pollutants. A lot of this material was getting into streams, and in West Marin most streams feed into Tomales Bay—an estuary whose special value was beginning to be recognized. Among other things, the bay is a major shellfish producer, and pollution from the watershed was shutting down the oyster harvest for months each winter.

What the water quality people had on the table, early in 1973, was a requirement that farmers build drainage systems and ponds to collect and contain runoff from barns and barnyards, even through the wettest part of the year. Then, in dry periods, the waste could be sprayed on pastures, where its nutrients (mostly nitrogen) would do some good and little harm.

All very reasonable, on paper. But could it be done on the ground? Unlike most other California dairying areas, Marin is all hills; it also gets more rain than most. Nor could some prefab system be applied across the board. Each dairy was a special case, with its own slopes and valleys, arrangement of buildings, and so on. Many dairies had been built on streams for the very purpose of

Starting to talk

convenient waste disposal; for these, the expense of ending pollution might be too much to bear.

As word of the proposed regulations spread, several details added to the basic alarm. One was the target set—not greatly reduced discharge, apparently, but none at all—"dreamlike," a critic said. Another was the timetable, or rather the lack of one: it appeared that the new requirements would apply immediately. (Rumored penalty for noncompliance: up to $6,000 a day.) And then there was this daunting fact: although the state was bound to enforce the standards, it was not prepared (or even permitted by law) to give any advice as to how they could be met.

Supervisor Gary Giacomini recalls thinking, "These people just don't understand. We can talk to them. We'll say, give us three or four years—the county will help; we want clean streams just as much as you do but if you make this effective immediately, it'll wipe these guys out." In March, a delegation of officials and ranchers went to Los Angeles to argue this case.

"And there was this huge hall, it would hold two or three thousand people, I guess. There were seven of us in the room, this little Marin contingent. The board said, 'What do you want?' I got up and made this impassioned speech. And the guy said, 'Are you through? We have enough milk anyway.' And they voted seven to zero to impose the rules instantly.

"The ranchers saw this as a gargantuan conspiracy. They thought, 'Great, the county comes along and zones us A-60. Now we're trying to do our thing and along comes the state and makes it impossible to do what it is we're zoned for.'"

Looked at from today's perspective, the rules adopted by the state seem not unreasonable. The language is clear but general. No deadlines are set or penalties mentioned. Details are entrusted to the Regional Water Quality Control Boards, more local and accessible bodies. But plainly the state authorities gave the impression that they didn't care, one way or another, about the ranchers' survival; the ranchers feared the worst.

Giacomini: "They thought it was flat impossible to design a system that would work on a two-thousand-acre ranch. They thought the state was saying, See you later, you don't get to be in business any more."

One of the more abstruse bureaucracies in California is a body called the California Milk Stabilization Board. Its job is to direct milk production toward areas of high demand and to prevent abuse of the virtual monopoly certain big creameries enjoy (if unregulated, they could pay ranchers as little as they chose). Under board rules, each dairy rancher has a milk quota, which is a valuable salable property, rather like a liquor license. A dairyman who wants out of business will, as his first move, offer his quota for sale.

In the week after the Water Resources Control Board met in Los Angeles, five ranchers let it be known that their quotas were for sale. "For a week or two," Giacomini remembers, "the ranches were going like dominos. I thought we'd lose 'em all."

Alarmed, Giacomini met with the ranchers who were ready to sell and pleaded with them to delay. Would they hold off for three months, maybe six? They would. He went to his colleagues on the Board of Supervisors. Would they chip in with the ranchers' local Resource Conservation District in hiring an engineer, someone who would survey all seventy-odd affected dairies to determine what systems, at what cost, would have to be built? The board agreed.

Loafing barn at the McIsaac ranch. These barns were built to improve dairy waste containment but also to shelter cows in bad weather.

Engineer Rixon J. Rafter of the Soil Conservation Service got to work. Ranch after ranch he tramped, measuring, gauging, and puzzling. The problem in many cases was finding a site for a wastewater pond large enough to hold all the polluted runoff from livestock areas. "I had to be like a cabinetmaker sometimes to get the darned thing in there," he recalls. Where pond capacity was limited, ranchers would have to take an additional much more expensive step and build huge barns, "freestall" or "loafing," to house the herds in the rainy season. The bottom line was not good news. Cost of improvements, per ranch, would average $60,000; some owners would be spending two or three times that sum.

Rafter's work had the backing of the Regional Water Quality Control Board. Though it could not legally approve plans in advance, the board staff hinted strongly that the engineer's designs would be acceptable. The regional authorities, in general, were to mix a good deal of practical mercy with the strict justice of pollution control.

Meanwhile, Giacomini was searching for more direct ways to help the ranchers. State and federal aid programs were explored but didn't prove fruitful. Low-interest loans were considered but ran into technical problems. Finally in June 1974, the Board of Supervisors made a simple, dramatic offer: it would make outright grants to ranchers, amounting to one-quarter of the cost of each pollution-control system, spread out over five years. Total cost to the taxpayers would be some $2 million.

Such a subsidy program, today, would be politically scary. But those were more lavish years. The county's environmental groups, among others, lined up unanimously to support the expenditure. It was made with surprisingly little controversy. Al Poncia, the first rancher to sign a contract, remarked: "It's like the last straw being taken *off* the camel's back."

The Drought

Before that crisis was properly over, though, a second was under way.

In the autumn of 1975, the rains failed. The following winter was the driest in California in one hundred years, with precipitation at one-third of average levels. Week by relentlessly sunny week the realization grew: this could be trouble indeed, for ranches as much as for towns.

A milk cow drinks forty gallons of water a day. Thousands of gallons are needed to wash down barns and other surfaces. Ten thousand gallons a day is the very least a good-sized dairy requires. In drought, also, feed prices explode.

By August 1976, the springs and ponds of seventeen dairies had gone dry; they were hauling water, at a cost of $3,000 to $10,000 a month. A little rain fell around the middle of the month, but it was a mockery: too little to add to supplies, just enough to spoil the last nutritional value of the dry grass standing in the fields.

Meanwhile, the drought was also driving up the cost of the imported feed on which all local ranches depend. Between May and September the price of alfalfa (Arabic for "the best feed") had doubled.

The supervisors were again looking for a way to help. Legal restrictions forced the board to work in peculiar ways. "We may have stretched the law a

Stock pond in Chileno Valley

bit that time," Gary Giacomini says. But finally a way was found to pay half the cost of hauling water, $50,000 through that year.

November brought the official start of the rainy season but again no rain. There was talk of putting cloud-seeding installations on the ridges but there was scarcely a cloud to seed.

As rancher Boyd Stewart remarked to the press, "It sure would be a lot simpler to have some rain, wouldn't it?"

In January, a large ranch near Novato was the first to go under, its herd and quota sold. Appeals to Sacramento and Washington brought legislation and promises but not much in the way of actual relief. In April, the county increased its support of water-hauling costs to 75 percent. Soon the number of Marin County ranches importing the precious liquid was up to two dozen. The largest supply operation came out of the California Cooperative Creamery in Petaluma; eight or nine of its big silver milk trucks, with volunteer overtime drivers, would make two extra trips a day, water-laden. Ranchers' reservoirs tended to be in places the big trucks had trouble reaching; soon people were installing, as more accessible temporary ponds, inflatable plastic swimming pools.

The Milk-Price Hearings

Harsh though the drought was, it brought the real breakthrough in relations among the ranchers, their government regulators, and the conservationists whom they still regarded somewhat as their tormentors.

Soon after the seriousness of the drought became obvious, a new ad hoc group appeared on the scene: the Committee for Family Farms. One of its founders was Planning Commissioner Jerry Friedman. It set out to find ways of helping the farms survive.

One thing the dairy owners obviously needed was a boost in the prices paid them by the creamery for milk. These prices are controlled by both the state and federal governments (depending on what the milk is to be used for) in a system that not even ranchers seem to understand. The biggest factor,

Bob Giacomini's modernized milking parlor, Point Reyes Station

though, is the price set for plain milk, drinking milk, by the state Milk Stabilization Board.

In April, dairy farmers petitioned the state board for a three-cent-per-half-gallon price increase, emergency and temporary. Consumer groups, as expected, were opposed. But Friedman and the Committee for Family Farms had been busy. To Sacramento, with Gary Giacomini and the Farm Bureau, went the Environmental Action Committee; the Marin Conservation League; the Environmental Forum of Marin; the Inverness Association (a local community group); and, among organizations of larger scope, the statewide Planning and Conservation League and the international Friends of the Earth. And they went to say Yes to an increase.

"Something extraordinary is happening here today," Friedman told the Milk Stabilization Board. "There are people and groups testifying here . . . who have never before attended a milk-price hearing." Said Sue Jacob of the Environmental Action Committee, "Who ever thought I'd be fighting against consumer groups? That's weird. . . . But they just don't understand the concerns of family farmers." The state came through with part of the requested increase. It was, said Jacob, "the one note of encouragement in what otherwise looks to be a very discouraging year."

It did indeed. In May, the bridge on the old Nicasio road—vanished since 1960 under one of the county's major reservoirs—poked out of the receding water. Not long after, the lake bed was desert-dry. A newspaper photograph of the day shows, on the cracked mud at Nicasio, the skeleton of a carp.

Autumn arrived without rain, and many meteorologists predicted a third dry winter in a row. The authorities, having spent $280,000 so far, were gearing up for another year of disaster relief. The number of dairy operations in the county had dropped by another seven.

A Moment of Victory

November 20, 1977, dawned hazy and cool. As the day went on, sky, sea, and hills dimmed to a quiet gray. By late afternoon there was mist in the air. By nightfall, it was pouring. Within twenty-four hours, the storm had dropped

Nicasio Reservoir, after the drought

six inches of rain on Point Reyes Station. Upstream at Lake Nicasio, the reservoir reappeared on the cracked mud flats. In hours it had covered the old bridge. Out in the Pacific, another storm was bearing down. The rains were back.

And with this second crisis past, West Marin agriculture seemed to have proved itself. So had the policies designed to sustain it. Several strange things, undreamed of in 1970, had in fact occurred.

First, the county had spent money on the ranchers. Quite a bit of money. On two occasions. This fact impressed people in the farm belt as nothing else could have done. The old resentment—the feeling of being "used," of being required to provide public open space for free—at last began to subside.

Second, the awkward tentative convergence of 1973, when ranchers, conservationists, and county officials had first started setting out common ground, had developed into what can only be called an alliance. The difficult times had tested it as easier ones might not have. Leaders had gotten to know each other, confirmed their common interest in maintaining farm use, found ways of defusing issues that might have sprung them apart. And the county had come to perceive its farms as valuable in themselves, not merely as part of a land-use strategy: to hold them, indeed, in honor.

The psychological turning point, for many, had been the milk-price hearings. When speakers from environmental groups made their supportive statements, the farmer-dominated audiences would stand up and cheer.

"In a way," Jerry Friedman remarks, "we were lucky that there was a crisis. Up until that point there wasn't too much environmentalists could do to prove that we were serious about helping them stay in business."

On a tour of a ranch near Point Reyes Station, another planning commissioner marveled: "If someone had told me four or five years ago that the Marin Conservation League would follow ranchers around their properties without somebody getting shot at, I'd have thought they were crazy."

Third, the dairies that survived emerged considerably stronger. The new pollution systems incidentally gave them a source of fertilizer they had not used before. The numerous new barns kept cows healthier and more productive in the muddy winter months and reduced wastage of feed. Even the wells and ponds many had added during the drought made operations more secure. And the final result of the milk-price campaign was a new formula system for setting prices, one that would respond automatically without delays or lobbying when farmers' costs went up (or, indeed, down). That helped, too.

But most important of all, the troubled times had forced decisions. Faced with so much expense, so many hard choices, each dairy family had been forced to declare itself out—or in. Most stayed in.

Back at the A-60 hearings, agricultural economist William Wood had remarked on the dilemma of the farmer who owns land: "He is a land speculator whether he likes it or not. He is ambivalent." But however attracted some had

Baled hay in Chileno Valley

been in the past to the thought of a real estate windfall, West Marin ranchers were, when they got right down to it, more farmers than speculators.

Anybody in West Marin today will tell you that dairying is a hard business; many think about getting out; some do. And many have fears about the future. But since 1978 the old dark question, "Is ranching really viable in Marin, now, today?" has simply not been asked.

PROFILES

The Water Harvest:
Mary Dolan and Martin Strain;
John Vilicich (Tomales Bay)

Not all the livestock managed in Marin County is the warm-blooded, air-breathing kind. Into the middle of agricultural Marin, splitting its greens and yellows with a track of blue, comes water, salt water, Tomales Bay; and out on the water other farmers gather other yields: the fishermen and the shellfish-raisers, agriculturalists of the sea.

Long, thin, straight, and shallow, Tomales Bay has no obvious reason for being there. It marks, not the mouth of the "very great river" its Spanish discoverer guessed at, but an even mightier feature, the San Andreas Fault. Very *small* rivers, the county's largest creeks, do converge on it. Papermill or Lagunitas Creek, dammed to satisfy the thirst of cities "over the hill," pours diminished flows into its head, and Walker Creek, whose tributaries sprawl through half the cow lands, enters it near the mouth.

Like every estuary, Tomales Bay is a nursery for ocean life and a passageway for anadromous fish like salmon. Like very few estuaries near cities, it is still nearly unpolluted. Though not unchanged—sedimentation and reduced freshwater inflow have done damage and probably continue to do so—the bay has reached the 1990s in better condition than any other sizable estuary between Mexico and Oregon.

Ask Mary Dolan and Martin Strain, who grow oysters and mussels on state tidelands north of Marshall. "Ours is an industry that requires a very clean environment to survive," says Strain. "We've got that here—so far."

Strain has roots in West Marin. His grandparents owned a dairy ranch near Dogtown (now part of Point Reyes National Seashore). But Martin grew up in Stockton, graduated from the University of California, Berkeley, and went to

Herring dock on Tomales Bay

Ken Taylor rowing to his mussel beds

work in San Francisco as an accountant. That lasted only till he had some savings to gamble with. In 1984, he made his move.

At that time, the state's process for leasing tidelands was pretty informal. You could study the waterscape, pick your site, and ask officialdom to agree. Strain got the plot he wanted: five acres near the midpoint of the eastern shore, a location where the water is fairly deep and particularly clean.

Aquaculturists' terms are like farmers'—"seed," they say, and "harvest." Dolan and Strain buy their oyster seed—technically, "quarter-inch graduates"—from a Eureka nursery in the spring. They place the tiny creatures in big mesh envelopes (about half a cup, maybe two hundred oysters, per bag) and attach the containers to long ropes strung out like clotheslines in the tidal zone. Harvest begins in about nine months.

Oysters don't, of course, need to be fed, but they do need continual tend-
ing, mainly to make sure they don't get crowded and assume odd forms.
"They're amazing contortionists," says Martin. "If you had a doughnut-
shaped container, you would get a doughnut-shaped oyster. When we had
them in trays, they'd grow into perfect squares in the corners." That's no triv-
ial matter if you are selling, as this company does, to the half-shell market:
customers demand not just good meat but also a perfect, symmetrical shell.

Although Strain and Dolan call themselves the Pt. Reyes Oyster Company,
their favorite critter is actually the mussel. When they took up business, there
was no such thing as commercial mussel seed; you just set up habitat—pil-
ings wrapped in burlap, for instance—and hoped that free-swimming mussel
larvae, or spat, would attach. "We had absolutely no luck with that." Re-

Tim Hollibaugh, Tomales Bay oyster grower and marine biologist

cently, mussel seed has come onto the market, and Dolan and Strain are learning the ropes of this second, very different, crop.

Oysters are proper produce. They stay put. Mussels are livestock. They can stray. They attach themselves to surfaces with tough tendrils called byssal threads. "If life is too rough where they are," says Mary, "the mussels just cut their threads and move somewhere else." Martin goes on: "They emit another kind of thread, a weblike one that helps them float in the current. They can drift along for miles until they think they've found a better place to settle." The first year the company grew mussels, it seeded them too densely, and many disappeared. "I hate to think how many millions we lost."

Again unlike oysters, which grow loose in their fine mesh bags, the almost microscopic mussels are first established on fibrous substrate (rope is good). Then fragments of substrate are placed in bags of much coarser mesh. As the animals mature, they arrange themselves to protrude through the mesh in solid ranks, filtering food from the current outside. To collect them, "you grab the top edge of the mass with your hands, outside the bag. They come off in big sheets as you pull your hands down the bag." After the first such harvest, immature mussels from inside the bag move out to build a second lavish layer. "Like a pelt," says Mary. "Like a huge black pearl necklace," Martin puts in.

More than most other companies (there are six now on the bay) Strain and Dolan take their live products directly to the consumer "over the hill." They sell at farmers' markets—San Rafael twice a week, Davis on Saturdays; they do oyster bars for caterers; they supply to restaurants. "Selling is the most time-consuming part of all."

Good as Tomales Bay is for the shellfish farmer, one thing would make it better: a truly pristine watershed, with no people and no cows. A number of times a winter, during and just after rainstorms, harvest is stopped for fear of contamination from faulty septic tanks and—despite heavy investments in pollution control on the ranches—from cow manure. Shellfish, "filter feeders" that comb organic bits out of large volumes of water, concentrate whatever undesirable bacteria they take in; they cannot be sold until they've had time to clean themselves out—up to six days after the rain stops. One solution is to build a holding tank in which clean oysters can be stockpiled to bridge these gaps, but that's a major expense.

If ranching were to cease in the Tomales Bay watershed, though, the probable alternative—not wilderness but large-scale urban development—would be far more damaging. Human waste is a greater threat than animal manure, and much worse than either are the exotic effluvia of the modern city: pesticide residues, petroleum products, cadmium, mercury, lead . . . once shellfish ingest these substances, they get rid of them very slowly or not at all. For this reason, Martin Strain has spoken out against a plan to discharge urban sewage from Santa Rosa, however highly treated, into the Estero Americano, just outside the Tomales Bay mouth. "It might be all right at first," he says, "but as Santa Rosa gets more industrial, God knows what could wind up in the bay."

Few people know Tomales Bay as well as John Vilicich, fisherman, boatbuilder, and local institution. The son of Dalmatian immigrants, he was born in 1919 on Tomales' western shore. He has fished within its mouth for herring and perch, and in the ocean outside it for salmon, sea bass, rockfish, halibut,

John Vilicich, owner of the Marshall Boat Works

and crab. He's seen these waters day and night, safe and hazardous, stormy and calm. He's seen the estuary blue and sharply saline in drought years, muddy and roiled and creekwater-fresh at the surface in seasons of flood. He's seen the number of bay-based boats and fishermen multiply. And he's seen the rise of the rules.

Seasons. Stickers. Permits. Net specifications. Fees. And quotas: "When the quota is caught, boom, the season is over." In general, Vilicich doesn't mind. "I like the water. I want to save the resource. Most fishermen do. That's the deal."

He's quite content, for instance, with the new regulation about crab pots (he has about a hundred pots, outside the bay mouth). They must now be tied shut with cotton, not synthetic, line. If for some reason a pot isn't picked up, the line will rot and release the crab that's inside. And Vilicich is not opposed, though some fishermen are, to new regulations governing the use of gill nets. These efficient and selective nets trail strands that entangle the gills of larger fish—but can also trap marine mammals and such diving birds as murres.

Vilicich hasn't lived by fishing alone. Since 1946 (when he got out of the Navy) he has operated the family boatyard at Marshall, in recent years with the help of his son and partner, Ed. The yard is now the largest repair operation between Sausalito and Ford Bragg. "We don't have to fish real hard," he says, "because we have the income from the yard."

As you might expect of a boatbuilder's boat, Vilicich's *Miss Marin* is full of the latest electronic gear: a depth finder (helpful in crossing the unpredictable Tomales bar); Loran navigation system; CB and VHF radios; direction finder and high-tech compass; a recorder that picks up the characteristic sounds of herring and anchovy schools. One elaborate piece of gear tests water temperatures and shows them as swirls of color: "It tells us how hot the water is." "Hot," to a fisherman—to an oyster grower, as well—is anything over about 55 degrees.

John Vilicich is nervous these days about the future of the bay he knows so well. Over the years, he's seen the catches of the various species fall and rise and fall again. He's seen the steady decline of salmon and the disappearance of striped bass. He's seen the annual herring catch drop from two or three thousand tons in the 1930s to nine hundred tons—in an exceptional year—today. And though the numbers bounce around from year to year, obscuring the overall trend, he's lately become convinced that the downhill slide is lasting and real.

A lot of people around Tomales Bay agree. Some put the blame on overfishing, some on agricultural practices in the watershed, some on events outside the region. (All, no doubt, have a case.) But what is hurting the bay most, Vilicich maintains, is the loss of freshwater inflow from its feeder streams, diverted for urban water supply. An estuary, by definition, is where salt water mixes with fresh; there are years when Tomales Bay barely qualifies. Herring, notably, hatch poorly when the brine is too briny. "Before the herring season, I keep asking, 'Is the old Nicasio Dam running over yet?' By February, it's too late. Salt water pickles the eggs."

Everybody knows the story of the miner's canary, the sensitive bird that's used to test doubtful underground air: if the canary lives, people can breathe, too. Aquaculture, so vulnerable to pollution, is a little like that bird. So is the fishing industry. Between them, the two indicators give a mixed report on Tomales Bay. A yellow light, perhaps. Something less than a clean bill of health. They show us a bay in good shape now, as modern American estuaries go, but by no means to be taken for granted.

Don't look away.

The Recruit: Gordon Thornton (Tomales)

What's the best thing about ranching? Put that question to just about any rancher in Marin, and you'll get the same two answers: "You are your own boss." And: "It's a great way to raise kids."

But kids get older. Parents, too. And sooner or later, the ranch family faces the problem: who'll be next? where is the next boss coming from? The days are gone when the oldest boy was expected, automatically, to stay; nobody wants to lobby the youngsters; but the pressure is there, built in.

And what if there isn't a child (ordinarily still, a son) who wants the job? It's sad all around. But in many such cases, a heartening thing occurs. Somebody else comes forward, an in-law maybe or a city-bred grandson, who is happy to take on the ranching trade, headaches and all: provided only that the land itself has not meanwhile been sold.

Gordon Thornton of Tomales is one of the breed—urban members of ranch-owning families who find they have not, after all, left the rural world behind. Great-granduncle James Marshall was one of five brothers who came to Tomales Bay in the 1850s, bringing with them, overland from Kentucky, the county's first shorthorn dairy cows. At one time the Marshalls owned twelve square miles along the bay. What's left today is one splendid spread, the original home ranch, on a green plateau above a bend of Walker Creek.

Gordon and Dan Thornton, Tomales.
"It's being your own boss. You and the
feed company and all that."

"I'm the first one to own this land," says Thornton, "who's not actually named Marshall."

Gordon did most of his growing up in a tract house in Santa Rosa. But he did an important bit of it here on the Walker Creek place, working, weekends and summers, for his Marshall uncles. Neither uncle had ranch-minded children, and many years later, when the labor got to be too much for them, Gordon was the obvious successor—if he chose to give up a secure position at PG&E. He chose.

When Gordon began managing the ranch, about the only immediate change he made was to buy a new bailer. "The uncles always bought second-hand bailers." He grins. "I still have that bailer. But at least I know what goes wrong with it. Because you grow together, you know."

Disagreements inevitably arise when ranch management is shared between generations—or when it is shared at all. "A lot of times you'd like to do things different, and if you do   sometimes it's better, sometimes the old way was just as good. Or better. You have to try it to find out."

*Shearing break at the Thorntons'. Tim
Furlong, neighbor, and J. P. Butler
(right), New Zealand sheepshearer.*

Most Marin ranches are dairies or livestock operations, one or the other. Thornton's is both. He runs about eight hundred sheep and some twenty beef cattle and also milks ninety-five cows—a herd maybe half the size of the typical one, too small to be economical by itself, but in his mixed operation a mainstay. "Beef was down last year. Wool was poor. But lamb prices were real good, and milk was steady. . . . You don't have to milk a lot of cows," he adds. "Just milk *good* cows."

Milk, beef, lamb, wool . . . there's a fifth major product here, one that's consumed on the spot. "We put up maybe fifty or sixty tons of oat hay. And a couple of hundred tons of grass hay." The crop is planted in the fall, in a gamble with the weather. If it goes into the ground too early, there may not be enough rain to establish the crop. Too late, and it may be too cold. "I like to plant the oats before Thanksgiving. After Thanksgiving, you wonder if they'll ever come out of the ground."

In the old days this ranch, like the country for miles around, was planted to wheat and potatoes—and not just on gentle slopes like Thornton's. "Anywhere a horse could stand, they'd plow. The ground was fairly fertile, they got some good crops for a few years." Then as now the technique was to plant just before the rains and hope; but on steeper ground a too vigorous early storm could wash ditches in the field.

Gordon has an eye for erosion problems. With fellow ranchers Leroy Erickson and Mervin McDonald, he serves on the Marin board of the Agricultural Stabilization and Conservation Service, a federal agency that makes small grants for erosion control and other purposes (it also helped out when dairies were building their wastewater systems). As part of the deal, ranchers who receive such money now agree not to farm overly steep terrain.

On Keys Creek at Tomales, when it was a navigable waterway, stood a potato warehouse. When the potatoes stopped coming, the building was taken apart and moved to the Marshalls' hilltop. It is now a Thornton barn. Its timbers, pegged and morticed, some of them handhewn, are heart redwood, one foot square. "Even if you could get beams like this today, you couldn't afford to buy 'em."

Gordon Thornton is not sorry his summons to the land came a little late. "It's good for a person to work somewhere else," he thinks. "Then you know what you *do* like."

For one more generation, at least, it seems the Thornton ranch is secure. Gary, one of Thornton's two sons, has "gone partners" with his father. When Gordon knew that for sure, some years ago, he built a new Grade A dairy barn.

A Family of Farms: Earl and Micky Dolcini
(Marshall—Petaluma Road)

When he was growing up on the Brown ranch in Hick's Valley, Earl Dolcini thought his was the poorest family in the world. He was helping out in the barn at age eight. "Sometimes," he recalls, "the milk check was really rotten."

Now he sees that part of his life in a little more perspective. No refrigerator, "but we ate everything in sight." No luxuries, unless you count fresh vegetables and venison. Not much money, but somehow the family managed to do what the Dolcinis have been doing for a century or more: acquire additional land.

Earl's great-grandfather, Carlos Martinoia (later Charles Martin), came here in 1852, via Africa and France, from the same small area that fountained out so many of Marin's dairy families: the rocky valley of the Maggia River, tucked up among the southern Alps in the Swiss canton of Ticino. A belated '49er, Carlos tried milking gold from the Sierra foothills but soon enough "came back to the cows." He worked with other people's animals for a time, then got onto his own land. He raised seven children and bought an additional ranch for each of the three boys. One of the daughters, Earl's grandmother, Anita, married another recent arrival from Valle Maggia, Peter Dolcini. They, too, set about buying land.

Thus far the story is traditional, lived out with variations in dozens of local dairy families. What makes the Martin-Dolcini tribe stand out is the ownership arrangement. For well over a century, most of the land that has come into the hands of Charles's descendants has been treated as a single common holding. The eight Marin ranches now in the family don't belong to this or that branch of it: they simply belong to the family, in one great multispoked partnership, the interest undivided. Anybody who has ever had a relative can think of possible difficulties, and the family has weathered its share. "You don't keep property together for 130 years," says Earl proudly, "unless there is a pretty strong core of understanding and willingness to work together."

In 1960, Earl and Micky Dolcini—and their five young children—moved onto the big half-wild property known as the League ranch, in the Salmon Creek Valley along the Marshall–Petaluma Road. In terms of modern conveniences, it could almost have been the Brown ranch again: no gas or electric power, no telephone, and a tall old house that, though handsome and distinctive, needed endless restoration. And got it: the place gleams. Around it Micky has drawn a cool patio and garden. "When we came here," she remembers, "there was one tree."

The days are gone when choosing to live in rural Marin meant choosing isolation. The Dolcinis find it delightful to be so close to San Francisco, and meetings and errands may take them daily into local towns. Earl spends much of his time at board meetings of the Western Farm Credit Bank, of which he is a district director. He recently ended a stint as chairman of the Marin Agricultural Land Trust (MALT). Micky, like most country moms, spends dozens of hours each month at the wheel of a car—driving inland among the hills to Petaluma and Novato, driving west again, ferrying her youngest daughter, Becky, to and from school, attending meetings of her own. Among other interests, she's a charter member of the St. Anthony Farms Auxiliary. (The farms are the rural arm of the St. Anthony Foundation, best known for its St. Anthony Dining Room in San Francisco; forty men grow food for the dining room and get help in dealing with addiction problems at the same time.)

The Dolcini youngsters, of whom there are now eight ("we raise beef and kids on this ranch," Earl says) have developed their own strong feeling for the country. "They also realize that this isn't going to be in the future for every one of them." Grandpa probably did it, but in today's real estate market there's no way a modern rancher can endow a large next generation with land. Because division can threaten—or destroy—a farm business, Dolcini is absolutely opposed to splitting properties.

Besides the current home ranch, Dolcini runs a dairy operation on the same Brown ranch where he spent his childhood. He is one of a very few dairymen hereabouts who milk Jersey cows. Jersey milk, higher in butterfat and solids

Earl Dolcini, dairyman and head of the Dolcini clan, Hick's Valley. "If the public stays with us, agriculture will survive."

than other breeds', is out of favor for drinking; it does yield a sweet and flavorful skim milk.

Earl recalls how the extrarich milk used to bedevil a local cheesemaker. "They would put a standard amount of milk in each container to make their little Camemberts. And all the cheeses made from our milk would come out too big." But today he has a steady customer in the Marin French Cheese Factory, two fields away from his dairy barn. "We even get a little premium payment now."

Ex discrimine ad discriminem reads a Latin motto hung on the wall at the Dolcini home. "From crisis to crisis." Dairy ranchers have always lived by that law, but these days the business seems only to get more intense. During deer season, Earl will sometimes go up on the hillside with his gun and try to recapture the boyhood pleasure of hunting. "I sit down and it's nice and quiet and the first thing you know I'm thinking of thirty-three things I should be doing and I'm not enjoying it so much any more."

Something else that makes him uneasy is the fear that urban development, confined now "over the hill," may yet come spilling into the dairy belt. High land prices, with the pressure and temptation they bring, are worrisome. "You can't be hoping to cut a fat hog at some point and at the same time be a dedicated rancher. You're either a rancher, or you're not a rancher."

In the early 1970s, he remembers, there was a plan to put thirty-two houses on a ranch in Hick's Valley opposite the cheese factory. "I dropped everything and said, 'What are we going to do about this?'" He wrote the Planning Commission warning that, if the housing project were approved, the Dolcini family would request three thousand acres of residential zoning on their comparable nearby lands. He also challenged the developer's environmental impact report, which suggested that the project would add just 1.6 pupils to one-room Lincoln School. "Maybe there's something different about this area that you haven't considered," Dolcini told the Board of Supervisors. "Three of us brothers live in this valley, and we have twenty-one children among us." He laughs his quiet laugh. "It took four minutes to restore order." Soon the controversial property was zoned A-60, matching the surrounding land.

Urban development, he acknowledges, has to happen, as long as it stays within bounds. He grins, "We've got to have all those milk drinkers live *somewhere.*"

Four ■ SOMETHING MORE PERMANENT?

Drought over. Pollution control systems going in. Milk prices unstuck . . .

With these immediate emergencies past, the new three-way alliance of ranchers, conservationists, and government people could look a little farther ahead. What could be done to make certain that the work done would not some day be undone? How could the accomplishment be ensured?

"The Terror I Have"

The future of West Marin is not in West Marin's hands. With 5 percent of the county's population, the region depends on policies made "over the hill," in the county government building known irreverently, despite its famous Frank Lloyd Wright design, as Big Pink. Even the supervisor who represents West Marin has far more constituents on the urban side of "the hill." Given a change in political climate, new faces on the board, a new list of crises, the old policies could erode, bit by bit or even very rapidly.

To be sure, it hadn't happened yet. In the first five years after A-60 zoning was enacted, the Planning Commission and the Board of Supervisors had never budged on its enforcement. Word got around, and after one or two early probes, applicants stopped trying. The deadly game of exceptions and creeping redefinitions, fatal to many a well-laid plan, never got started. Yet local zoning can be undone, legally speaking, in a hurry. Given a five-member governing board, all it takes is three votes and thirty days.

"The terror I have," says Giacomini: "it's five years from now, and it's all down the drain. I'm always worried that a development menu will be served

Warren Weber, specialty vegetable grower, Bolinas

up rich enough in property taxes to attract three of five supervisors. It could happen. Any Tuesday, three to two: A-60 is gone."

One defense, plainly, was to keep the leaders and voters of eastern Marin interested in West Marin's agriculture, both for its own sake and as part of the structure of the countywide plan. In 1978, the Farm Bureau and the Environmental Forum of Marin put together the first Family Farm Day, an annual event ever since. Each year urban folk troop out "over the hill," tour several ranches, consume a barbecue, and get an earful about how the rancher's life works day to day. The organizers take care to invite every decision maker they can get their hands on, local, state, and even federal. Many come.

Another defense—never much discussed in Marin—lies with the voters. If a board of supervisors did start to weaken A-60, citizens could take direct control and enact a similar zoning ordinance at the polls. Such things have been done. Once passed, an initiative measure of that kind could be reversed or changed only by another popular vote.

By the end of the 1970s, however, it had become apparent that merely holding the line, standing by past policies, was not going to be enough.

Willie Bird turkeys, Tomales. "We came to Marin for the cool weather," says Willie Benedetti. "Turkeys lay better here."

The Ranchettes Are Coming

When sixty-acre zoning was first adopted, the county assumed that, by permitting subdivisions with sixty-acre "lots," it was in effect ruling out any development at all. Nobody, it thought, would buy sixty acres simply for a backyard. The actual urban density would be what advisors assured the county was needed for the good of agriculture: *zero.*

Times change.

In the late 1970s, a new kind of customer began shopping for land in Marin County. Someone with ties to the city but not tied down to a daily commute. Someone in love with horses, windy landscapes, and winding roads. Someone with money to spare, for whom the cost of buying sixty acres as a private preserve was not daunting.

The pressure was felt first on the inland edge of the farm belt, near Nicasio. In 1978, two ranches near Nicasio Reservoir were divided into parcels of near-minimum size. The county's environmental impact report called the proposal "inconsistent" with county planning goals and "irrevocable" in impact. Nevertheless, the supervisors felt they had no choice but to go along.

A new anxiety went through the ranching community. A non-rancher may well wonder why. What could be more charming than a rural "ranchette," sleek and inconspicuous, with a couple of glossy horses wandering around the fields?

Yet there was reason for alarm. Several reasons, in fact.

First, the sudden appearance of a market for 60-acre parcels could only drive up land prices in general, pushing acreage farther out of the reach of agricultural buyers. More land would be drawn out of the purely agricultural land market, with its fairly modest prices, into a much richer game.

Second, long experience shows that "ranchettes" mix very poorly with commercial agriculture around them. Agriculture, real agriculture, is always a somewhat messy business. There is mud. There is dust. There are noises, smells, and flies. There are slow vehicles monopolizing roads. There may be chemical sprays. The new rural landholders, unaccustomed to these things, have a natural instinct to "improve the neighborhood." And they're likely to be people who know how to proceed. In one extreme Marin County case, a buyer purchased a slice of a major ranch, then sued the seller to prevent him from keeping pigs on the remainder. After a long wrangle, the exhausted rancher gave up and moved away.

Annoyance runs in the other direction, too: youngsters from the ranchettes, untrained in the rural codes, are likely to trespass, break down fences, leave open gates that should be closed, or, less innocently, vandalize objects and harass stock. Then there are the dogs, scarcely less a problem to West Marin ranches than coyotes are. Rover and Fido, tame at home, revert in the hills to the hunting animals they are; in one year, a dog near Tomales killed over fifty lambs.

Around the nation, the intrusion of ranchettes into true farm areas has often been the beginning of the end. From government's point of view, low-density rural development has the further disadvantage that it costs far more in services (especially school for the kids) than it yields in property taxes.

So A-60 zoning—once denounced as a tyranny, later accepted as a good and sufficient shield—now began to seem merely weak. "In 1972," Gary Giacomini recalls, "A-60 seemed outrageously profound. Looking back later, we saw it as infantile." Back then, the county counsel had advised against

Abandoned chicken sheds near Tomales

Stewart ranch

Back in 1973, when a Marin
delegation worried that water
pollution rules would hurt local
dairy ranches, a state official re-
portedly shot back: "We have
enough milk anyway." That
comment was more than true.
Nationwide, the dairy industry
has long had a tendency to over-
produce and to damage its own
interest in doing so.

In the past, the federal government has supported the industry by maintaining a standing
offer to buy at fixed prices such
storable products as butter and
cheese. In 1985, impatient with
the expense of this program and
the stockpiles of dairy products
that were accumulating, Congress passed a law that reduces
the guaranteed level somewhat
every year. The state is involved
in price setting, too; its formula
responds to the federal one. All
in all, dairies are getting less
money for what they produce.

But just as the generous subsidies of the past encouraged
production, so, seemingly, do the

setting a higher minimum size, for fear of trouble in court; now many wished
that the risk had been taken.

What to do? There was some talk of an increase in minimum lot size to two
hundred acres, or four hundred, or six hundred. Lots on such a scale are large
enough to be independent farms and to circulate in the agricultural land market. And zones of very large parcels have in fact become common tools in
California zoning since A-60 first raised eyebrows. Another option would be
to abandon the crude tool of parcel size and aim more directly at the target: set
up an exclusive agriculture zone in which non-farming development would be
prohibited outright.

If any such change were to be made, 1979 was a logical moment to get
started on it. Under a revised state coastal planning law, which in 1976 had
replaced the voter-enacted system of 1972, Marin was preparing a special
Local Coastal Plan for lands along its western shore. Though only a fraction of
the county's farmland was actually in this strip, whatever was done there had
enormous precedent value. Stronger zoning for the coastline might later
spread inland; if coastal farmlands were not rezoned, it would be years before
the question could be raised again.

The ranchers, for their part, did not want it raised at all. As in 1972, even
while acknowledging development to be a threat, they opposed any further
cut in the potential for development. Their conservationist allies did not pur-
sue the matter. Having been through the bitter A-60 battle once and gotten
beyond it to an era of good feeling, they were not about to go back to the
beginning again.

The result (to skip ahead a bit) was a Local Coastal Plan that modestly
strengthened A-60 zoning; it required clustering of any residential development that might occur and set up standards testing all other proposed uses for
their effect on agriculture. But it left the basic density intact.

"Something More Permanent"

But if downzoning was not the answer, what was?

Two people who chewed over that question during these years were Phyllis
Faber and Ellen Straus, the co-founders of Family Farm Day. Faber had served on

the North Central Regional Coastal Commission; Straus was the Marshall rancher and conservationist who, with her husband, Bill, had been the first rancher actually to support A-60 zoning. "But zoning just isn't enough," Straus kept saying. "We've got to have something more permanent." Somehow the land had to be put out of reach of non-farming development—for good.

One possibility: some government agency could simply buy the land, then lease it back to the former owners. Exactly this, in fact, had already been done in Marin, and on a large scale. Point Reyes National Seashore, a special case among parks, contains a number of working dairy ranches. In 1972, when the National Seashore was buffered with a second federal park, the Golden Gate National Recreation Area, the lease-back policy was extended. This solution does not perfectly satisfy anyone, however. No rancher ever really likes to lose the land, even if a lease-back follows. And when a working ranch is in a park, there's a natural tug-of-war between the economic purpose of the ranch and the park's job of preservation. In Marin, this tension has kept quite a few environmentalists, notably the local unit of the Sierra Club, from joining in with the rancher-conservationist alliance.

In wider terms, saving farmland by outright purchase is an expensive way to go, and one that has no value as a general model: there isn't enough money in government budgets to safeguard more than a tiny fraction of the country's threatened agricultural land in that way.

But if not outright purchase, what about paying ranchers to sign away the *development potential* of the land, and the development potential only?

Methods of doing just that thing have been commonplaces in the planning trade for years, though rather more talked about than practiced. The trick is to treat the "right" to develop a piece of land, at whatever density the zoning allows, as something separable from the land itself, something the owner can sell or give away. As part of the transaction, the landowner executes an easement preventing development on the original site forever. The detached development rights can then be dealt with in several ways. Most commonly they are simply extinguished, reducing the total development allowed in a region. This variation is known as purchase of development rights, or PDR. On the other hand, rights may be sold for use on a piece of land more suitable for development, *increasing* allowable density there. This is transfer of develop-

new financial pressures. To survive, each ranch must grow more efficient; the result is still greater output per cow. Dairy ranchers today dread innovations that will allow them to produce more milk; they know that, when the innovations appear, they will be forced to adopt them or fall back in the race.

So why worry about the health of one small dairy belt? Shouldn't it, if anything, be encouraged to fail?

The first and obvious answer is that these local farms are providing more than milk. Their second commodity, invisible and precious, is one that now perhaps we can name without offending anyone: regional open space. We can also note that Marin and Sonoma dairies, more than their inland competitors, embody an ideal that the nation claims to support: the small-scale family farm. Quite apart from the industry situation, here are reasons for hoping that these dairies don't fail.

The second answer has to do with how little we know. We tend to look at a snapshot of agriculture and assume that the

Nicholas sheep ranch near Tomales

future will be like the present, only more so. It doesn't work that way. Crops change. Technologies shift. Competition ebbs and flows. And these days a wild new influence—planetary climatic change—may be at work. The summer drought of 1988 slowed milk production in several regions and (along with some other factors) momentarily "solved" the milk surplus problem; if weather fluctuations become harsher, a predicted result of the greenhouse effect, the chronic surplus of milk could become an equally chronic shortage.

If the Marin-Sonoma dairy belt did go out of business, the land lost to agriculture, its production capacity might never be missed. But then again, someday, it might. This was once, after all, the leading dairy region in California. Inland dairies overtook it because hot climate

Five minutes old

ment rights, or TDR. From these two basics, elaborate (but still largely theoretical) systems can arise.

Traditional conservationists are nervous about these tools. They point out that a "right" to develop, as an absolute, is not present in law; government has the power to regulate development without trying to guarantee a profit for everyone. Nevertheless, the idea of property as the one surefire investment is now so rooted in the American mind that governments find life much easier if they can accommodate it, at least to a degree.

In 1978, Straus and Faber resolved to take up seriously the search for "something more permanent." Soon their focus narrowed to the idea of a local land trust: a private nonprofit corporation, not part of government; focused on farmland specifically, not land in general; and run in large part by the ranchers themselves. At the time, this formula was unique. Turning to acquaintances at a national land-preserving organization, the Trust for Public Land, the two women took a crash course in how to proceed. And they began to talk the idea up on both sides of "the hill."

It took a while. At a first meeting of farm and environmental leaders, in the fall of 1978, there was skepticism. The farmers asked to see case studies,

and cheap abundant federal water allowed them to grow alfalfa right next door. It's a safe bet that irrigation water will become more expensive, perhaps much more expensive. And urban growth in the inland regions is beginning to compete for farmland there as well. The cool coastal dairylands, with their spring-green unirrigated pastures, could yet regain some of their old importance.

The American dairy industry—like the country's agriculture overall—has been an almost embarrassingly powerful engine. Under the circumstances we have learned to think of as "normal"—benign climate, cheap water, fairly cheap energy, an endowment of fertile soil—the problem is, if anything, to throttle the machinery down a little. It does not follow that parts of the engine should casually be thrown away. That's what we do in effect when we permit good farmland of any type to vanish—forever.

numbers, details. And in truth, conservationists too had to think twice about the idea. It was a risk. "If this doesn't work," Faber acknowledged at the time, "we've missed the chance to push for stricter zoning through the Local Coastal Plan."

In February 1979 dairyman Ralph Grossi became Farm Bureau president. Like Al Poncia ten years before, he was part of a new generation, open to unfamiliar ideas. "Ralph really put it to the farmers," Faber recalls. "Either go for this, or we'll be in big trouble"—meaning tougher zoning. Meanwhile, the Trust for Public Land had come through with case studies showing how farm families in different situations might benefit from selling or even giving their A-60 development rights to a trust.

In July 1980, the Marin Agricultural Land Trust was formed. Grossi was president of its board. With him served Faber, Straus, and Gary Giacomini; ranchers Al Poncia, Earl Dolcini, Wilfred LaFranchi, and John Zimmerman; Rod Martinelli, an attorney from a ranching family; and Don Rubenstein, a lawyer with the California Coastal Conservancy. The job was under way.

"I'm not scared yet": Russell Sartori (Tomales)

When Russell Sartori was growing up, he had dreams of being a baseball player. Professional; major league, maybe. But when he got out of school, the home ranch near Tomales called, and he came.

The Sartoris have been at the ranch since 1903. Some things there haven't changed a lot since then. Russell Sartori and his father, Romeo, stand for a particular management style, one you might call perfectionist-conservative. They run a small herd on a lot of acres. They make maximum use of their own grass. They stay strictly out of debt. More than some of their colleagues, the Sartoris seem willing to have something older than the latest, something smaller than the biggest, something a bit back from the so-called leading edge.

Conventional wisdom says it takes two hundred cows today to make a living. The Sartoris manage with forty fewer. They do this mainly by relying entirely on native pasture in the three to five green months in the spring. "That's our bread and butter. . . . We're fortunate. We never had to sell a piece of land here and a piece of land there. We don't rent any extra land and in the spring we don't buy any extra feed."

The ranch has no loafing barn; cows stay on the land year-round. Fields so used require meticulous care. The Sartoris rotate their herds daily, a practice almost unheard of, so that each pasture gets a rest every second day. With 160 cows and 300 acres of prime grass, they can do that. In the muddy midwinter period, when the grasses are green but not yet strong, they keep the cows on well-drained upper slopes. To avoid mud problems around the barns, they've paved the areas where the animals congregate for supplemental feed and on their way to milking.

One of the great assets of the ranch is water, eight big springs on the upper slopes of the local hill. Pipes and gravity take the water where it's wanted. Even the drought of 1976–1977 did not affect the flow. (These high-elevation springs are common in West Marin, a curious result of local geologic structures.)

When Russell came back to the ranch, his life changed. "Once you get into ranch work, it's hard to meet people. You fall asleep during the date." Still, he notes, there are not too many single farmers. He married in 1986. His wife, Jodie, has her own demanding career as a computer consultant for the likes of Levi Strauss and the San Francisco Symphony. What with conflicting schedules, they sometimes hardly see each other during the week. "There has to be some give-and-take."

We set out on a tour of his barns, a gray-brown tiger cat trotting at our heels like a dog.

The milking barn: "It's the same one we had when my grandfather was in the business." He laughs at the fixtures, antiquated but lovingly maintained. "You'll never see anything like this ever again." The essentials are modern, though. He explains how the squidlike attachments that draw the milk are automatically sterilized after each use. "The sterilizer shoots hot water through it, shoots iodine through it, then more water, then it's ready to be used again."

The feed barn: "It's as clean as could be, you could eat off the floor, but it's just old-fashioned." Right now they feed all cows the same amount, but Sartori talks longingly of computerized systems that recognize each animal by a dangling electronic token and feed her a ration proportionate to her milk output.

The calf barn: the oldest building on the ranch, it has been here longer than the Sartoris have. "This is a barn dance barn, there's no doubt about that. But it's going to fall down if we don't replace it. It's too old and too far gone to try to repair." He glances up at its massive redwood beams. "We'll use the beams in another barn.

"Psht. Psht. Psht": he coaxes a calf to wobble toward us. The Sartoris pride themselves on scrupulous care of their calves and have the death rate down to 1 percent, considered phenomenally low. The Sartori calves are bedded on fir

Russell Sartori, fourth-generation
dairyman, Tomales

shavings over lime; in the first hours of life, they are warmed with heat lamps. "And I give them a little extra room." The ranch raises its own replacement heifers. "They know you. They're much more docile that way."

When Russell came back from college in 1978, the dairy business was booming. Government subsidies were high, and farmers everywhere were expanding. "They increased the price of milk to a range where everyone almost had to milk more cows. But," Sartori recalls, "some people were already saying, 'We're going to choke ourselves.' Most of the ranchers just laughed."

The result—a greater nationwide milk surplus—was predictable. Congress attempted to reduce it, not by cutting federal price supports but rather by adding another layer of incentives. First came the diversion program, which paid farmers for lowering production. "That was a bunch of crap. The big dairies that created the problem collected huge sums for not producing that milk, and the minute the program stopped they went back to the same high level."

In 1986 came the whole herd buyout program, which paid dairy ranchers to make the ultimate cutback—quitting business. That didn't work either; while a few struggling operators cashed in, others effortlessly picked up the slack.

What *would* work? Sartori thinks the key is not to bribe ranchers to produce less but rather to penalize those who produce more. Over a certain base level, for instance, federal price supports should not apply. "They never put a lid on it," he complains.

The current federal policy experiment involves a slow lowering of the basic support price for *all* milk produced. This is putting a squeeze on dairies, especially when feed prices are high. "If someone younger than myself (I'm thirty-two) wanted to get in the dairy business today—it's just a damned shame—he might be twice as good a dairyman as some in business now, but he just couldn't start in. Right now the price of milk is so low he'd have a hell of a time making a living."

In his own case, Russell Sartori is reasonably optimistic. "It's going to be a long haul. But I'm not scared yet."

The Farmhouse by the Freeway:
Jerry and Cory Corda (Novato)

In a sunlit meadow west of Novato a tiny olive tree is putting a short shadow
on the grass. Not far off, a homemade monument recalls an immigration: the
arrival here, a century ago, of Joseph and Adelaide Corda, formerly of the
Valle Verzasca, Switzerland. Then it was Ellis Island, a sooty cross-country
journey, a slow putting down of roots. Today the family is in its fifth American generation, and half a dozen ranches in northern Marin are run by Corda
descendants; you could walk all day in a pretty straight line and never leave
Corda land.

And if you *are* a Corda, you may have done that. Every year since 1979, the
family has held a sort of rambling reunion: a cross-country tramp that begins
at the Corda place (Robert's) on Novato Boulevard and wanders up hill and
down valley, past the Corda-built monument and the Corda-planted olive
tree, ending with supper at the Corda place (Henry's) on San Antonio Creek
five miles away. In 1984, the centennial of immigration, the walk was extended to cover all the Corda ranches: fifteen miles, that year.

The Corda place (Jerry and Cory's) north of Novato on the Marin–Sonoma
County line is like the rest and yet a little different. For one thing, the terrain
is gentler, with low hills and flat, winter-flooded wetlands bordering the
Petaluma River. The house is a handsome modern structure, all cathedral ceil-
ings and tall fireplaces, not in a rural mold. But most important is the difference you hear. This house, this ranch, are within carshot of Highway 101:
main street of the Marin–Sonoma urban corridor; commuter conduit; live
wire of urban growth. It hums with disquieting power.

Back in the early 1970s, when planners and politicians were rethinking the
future of Marin, they assumed until late in the game that this stretch, geo-
graphically part of the accessible eastern corridor, would urbanize. It seemed
inevitable. But when the plan was presented to the public, people insisted
that a rural gap be left between Novato and Petaluma. And the decision was
made to try. If it could be done, the region including the Corda ranch would
remain agricultural after all.

Jerry, Tom, Charisse, and Lester Corda of Novato. "It's not really the work is so hard," says Jerry. "But you're on call seven days a week." Chorus: "The hours!"

Surely, if the fragile political barriers that protect Marin County ranch land start to crumble, places like this will be among the hardest pressed. Close in, one expects to see effects of the "impermanence syndrome"—the foreboding that signals, Don't struggle too hard, don't improve too much; the city is coming anyway.

But Jerry and Cory Corda aren't buying any syndrome. Don't feel impermanent in the least. Raising a family and running a 260-cow dairy do not begin to use up their energy. Jerry is an officer of the Marin County Farm Bureau and

Chores for Charisse

head of the local volunteer fire department; Cory works with the North Bay Dairywomen, the California Women for Agriculture, and what sound like a dozen more committees in the farm community. (On the side, she's a self-employed mortgage broker.)

Cory's special urge is to teach: to buttress the future of the dairy belt by showing urban people, urban youngsters above all, what dairying is like, what it gives, how it feels. She has passed out ice cream on city streets in celebration of Dairy Month. She's exhibited cows of the four main dairy breeds on Petaluma Boulevard. She and Jerry have trucked their own big gentle Holsteins to a dozen local and not-so-local schools and welcomed busloads of visitors to their own barns. And, with friend and colleague Annette Grossi, Cory is training Marin and Sonoma teachers how to teach about ranching.

"What's wonderful," she says, "is watching the kids touch animals they've never been able to touch before."

(And with a little urging she'll recall her own introduction to livestock. How she came to visit Jerry on the ranch, that first important time, in an elegant suit, cream-colored, wool. How she found her date of the evening getting ready to bring a heifer through a difficult delivery. "'Will you help me?' he asked. 'I guess, if you'll show me what to do.'" Scratch one clean outfit. Enter one healthy calf.)

What impressed her most about ranch life was the family closeness, the sense of long stability. "My father was in the service. We traveled all over the world, but we never had any spot where you could have friends for years and years. . . . Meeting all Jerry's relatives was just remarkable." An inconspicuous plaque in the new living room, addressed as it seems to future generations, gives you the idea. The Corda House, it reads. Established 1984.

The Corda ranch, like many others today, is a multifamily enterprise. Jerry shares the work with his brother, Tom, and with his father, Lester, the actual owner. It was grandfather Fred who purchased the land in the 1950s as a "spare ranch," with the growing tribe in mind.

"And what am I going to do for *my* grandchildren?" Jerry wonders. At today's land prices, ranchers can't pick up spare acreages for the kids or the kids' kids. If a home ranch is lost, there is no substitute. "So many youngsters of my generation grow up and left, went off to be mechanics or whatever. And all of a sudden they realized that this was a better way of life. And they came back.

"But then there were the ones who couldn't come back, because they had sold the land."

And that's the kind of outcome that Jerry and Cory Corda are working hard to avoid—to make it easier for others, too, to avoid.

Trader in Tomorrows:
Wilfred LaFranchi (Nicasio)

It isn't easy being the first one down a road. Wilfred LaFranchi, dairy rancher at Nicasio, could tell you something about that. But after five years of meetings, hearings, paperwork, and expense, he and his family have secured the future of their 660-acre farm by means of the complex procedure, talked about for years in Marin but never before used here, known as transfer of development rights.

*Willie LaFranchi, Nicasio. "If I can
help it, I'm going to die here."*

If you've driven the Nicasio Valley Road northwest from the old town square toward the reservoir, you've seen the LaFranchi land. It's part of the rolling slope that rises to the right, punctuated with dark rock outcrops, swirled in spring with greens and purplish browns and washes of the low-growing flower called goldfields. The LaFranchi barns are inconspicuous in a draw, but the house sits on a knoll in the middle of their personal square mile. Not many views in the county can match theirs. "If I can help it," Willie LaFranchi says, "I'm going to die here."

But like many ranch operators, LaFranchi is not sole owner of the land he loves. Title is shared with two brothers, a sister, and five nieces and nephews: people with their own lives, some in faraway cities, and their own priorities. Split nine ways, the income from a dairy ranch does not glitter. And a generation from now, the number of owners would be twenty-three.

Most of the family wanted to see the ranch continue, but by the late 1970s the inevitable question—how could all these people get some profit from the land?—was looming very large.

The all too obvious thing to do was subdivide and sell. The LaFranchi land, like most of West Marin, is in the county's A-60 zone; it could legally be split eleven ways. And in the Nicasio basin, more than anywhere else in the farm belt, there is precedent for rural residential growth. The sunny valley, sumptuous to look at and not far from the urban fringe, has long attracted the commuting professional, the well-off retiree. Of sixteen dairy ranches in the Nicasio Valley in 1960, just three now remain, side by side on the slopes north and west of town.

In this environment, it was natural to ask: why fight it? Why not write Nicasio off as an enclave of ranchettes, and concentrate on saving other less compromised areas for basic agriculture? But the hundred or so valley residents did not feel that way. They wanted the farms to stay and, under county auspices, drafted a community plan that said so.

Among the tools listed in that 1979 plan was transfer of development rights (TDR), a means of moving permitted development from a sensitive site to another where it does less harm. By 1982 the LaFranchis began to see TDR as a way out of their dilemma. They turned for help to a planner who had been consultant on the Nicasio Community Plan: Matt Guthrie of the San Rafael firm Forsher and Guthrie . . .

Run the tape forward five years. The LaFranchis are to sign an agreement with the county forgoing, permanently, any right to develop their home ranch for nonagricultural use. Meanwhile, they have purchased another piece of land, on the other side of Nicasio, adjoining the village center. This site was formerly zoned for just two houses. But the county has rezoned the parcel to permit not two units but seventeen: the two "native" ones, ten more to replace the ones lost on the LaFranchi home ranch, and five additional as a bonus (needed to make the new development as profitable as simply splitting up the home ranch would have been). A precise development plan, putting most of the new houses next to the Nicasio village center, has gotten all its approvals. Guthrie estimates that the last of the new lots will have sold by 1993—a decade after the LaFranchis walked in his door.

Seemingly, everyone profits. The LaFranchis can look forward to some income. They also keep a ranch. So does the farm belt. A block of rolling hills remains a pleasure to look at. And the development that will occur, if not free of impact, adds people very carefully just where the village thinks they should be added.

Three cheers?

Three cheers don't do it—don't suffice to acknowledge the labor and persistence that led to this outcome. In the planning game, five years is a long time from idea to approval; ten years to wait for the last of the income is a very long time indeed. And as yet the family has seen little but red ink: the purchase price of the new land, planning costs, engineering studies, soil and water tests, an environmental impact report, permit fees, and on and on. And the time! Nobody kept track of how long the family members spent to get agreement among themselves. Then there were abortive negotiations with a developer who thought of buying the development potential outright. Then the realization that, to bring the deal off, the family itself would have to set up shop as a developer.

Stages: the lengthy search for a site near the village to which excess units could be moved. The meeting with the Nicasio neighborhood: brought into the picture early, it was generally in favor but had plenty of legitimate questions. The years of work with the county authorities: the planning staff, determined that this precedent-setting effort should be exemplary, wanted everything done in extra detail and by the book—and parts of that book had not been written yet.

To bring it off, five separate government actions had to be accomplished: the community plan was amended, the relevant zoning ordinance changed, a preliminary master plan accepted, the rezoning accomplished, and the precise development plan approved. Another set of procedures, not so complex but still substantial, attended the surrender of development rights on the home ranch. And it may be years before the family knows whether or not it has made a financially wise decision.

"We stuck our necks way out on this thing," says Will LaFranchi's brother Art, who has been very useful to his kin these last few years: he is a lawyer.

They stuck their necks out in their own interest. But in doing that they incidentally took on a large piece of work for the whole community. With any luck, this transaction should be a model, the first of many, the difficult prototype to be followed by other deals more smoothly and perhaps more cheaply assembled.

In the pure form of TDR, the land from which the units are removed and the land to which they are added need not be owned by the same people. Rather, the development rights—or "credits," as they might more accurately be called—can be bought and sold and applied wherever appropriate. If that kind of commerce begins to develop in Marin, TDR may mean a lot to the future of local agriculture.

If it all works out as the optimists surmise, let's not forget that there had to be a first time, and the first time wasn't easy. Let's not forget that some people named LaFranchi, by sheer determined doggedness, broke trail.

"Stewards, that's what we really are": The Ericksons (Tomales)

Is agriculture, the supposed salvation of West Marin, actually ruining the place? Some people think so. The species of ruin they have in mind is soil

Leroy Erickson, sheep and cattle rancher,
Tomales. "The way I look at it, we don't
really own the land."

erosion. The process, natural enough but speeded up with awful ease by human abuse of land, drains fertility from the ground and sends down silt to plug up local bays. The culprit they have in mind is overgrazing, especially along streams.

And indeed you don't need to travel too far in the rural zone, especially in the inland valleys and around Tomales, to spot some pretty impressive damage. Active gully systems—little branching badlands, with vertical, barren sides—are gnawing away in too many places. And there are steep hillsides, not necessarily gullied but just bare and battered from heavy livestock use, that are certainly shedding soil.

Matters have been far worse. Certainly nothing now going on can match the kind of erosion that stripped topsoil from the Tomales hills during the potato boom, or the soil loss that followed the ruthless nineteenth-century logging of Bolinas Ridge. In the mid-1800s, schooners could steam into Tomales town; by 1900, sediment from the watershed had pushed this shoreline miles outward.

Some observers doubt that *current* losses are really very much over the natural rates for this geologically unstable countryside. Others see in today's gullies the active ugly legacy of less careful times. Still others are convinced that bad practices, here and now, are doing much new harm.

In the end, the cause of degradation doesn't matter. Erosion—more than you'd like to see—is certainly happening. It is damaging farms and streams and bays. And—most important fact of all—it can be dealt with.

Ask Leroy and Agnes Erickson, who run cattle and sheep on three hundred fifty rolling acres north of Tomales on the Marin-Sonoma line. Or talk to their son Lee, an engineer trained in the complexities of erosion problems and their equally complex solutions.

Not that the ground we are bumping over now looks erosion-prone. So gradual are the slopes right here that Leroy can travel them at will in his aging truck. Shifting into compound low gear, he can even leave the wheel, letting the vehicle drive itself at a patient two miles an hour while he works in back, snipping open the fragrant bales and tossing out alfalfa with a long-tined American Gothic pitchfork. The cut baling wires accumulate on a metal rail.

Sheep—white-faced, black-faced, mottled—come surging toward us. Erickson's sheepdog, Spike, marked like a miniature Holstein cow, whimpers with excitement at his feet.

Between hay-tossing stops, Erickson points out old landslide scars on steeper ground across the way. "That bowl over there, I bet that happened hundreds of years ago, before there were any cattle around." In 1982, a memorable rainstorm shook down hillsides all over the county, indiscriminately in towns, on farms, and in wild watersheds. Erickson gestures at another example. "Those three slides slid out back then. How many times have these hills done that in millions of years?" Landslides, or "debris flows," as geologists like to call them, have been shaping this landscape since it emerged from the sea.

Gullies are different. Those you can control, though preferably not by the method, still occasionally used, of tossing in old tires. Several years ago, Erickson tackled his worst case. A minor seasonal stream had gouged out a vertical-walled cut and was expanding it, as such streams do, by cutting away at its headwall. He brought in rock to stabilize that face, fenced a streamside strip to keep his livestock out, and planted willows.

To see the result we go down on foot, through deep grass damp with fog, flattened here and there where deer have bedded down. "The quail like it in here, too." He points to the now-armored headwall. "There was a big waterfall here. The water just kept eroding it out and the bank kept tumbling in." He indicates the willows. "All you have to do is cut a willow switch and stick it into the ground, when it's moist. There's blackberry, too, the 'coons spread that. And we've thrown some prunings in here, you can see a few rosebushes starting." He looks around at his surprising little oasis. "It's healing up pretty well."

Such work costs. "There are probably three or four hundred dollars' worth of rock here, just for having it delivered. Plus our time and expense on the fence. It isn't enhancing our income at all. Not on a short-term basis, it isn't. I think long-term it will, because who wants to see a Grand Canyon up through here?"

Short-term versus long-term: there's the key.

Very modest subsidies can sometimes help to bridge the gap. The Agricultural Stabilization and Conservation Service, working through local Resource Conservation Districts, pays up to half the cost of projects like this of Erickson's.

Farther down the same streamcourse, Erickson shows me one of the ways in which even small-scale erosion can add to ranch expenses. Invisible in grass and brush is the narrow slot of an inner streambed. "It's a real hazard. A lot of times a cow will have her calf down in here. The calf'll stagger around and get down in the slot and you don't even see 'em. So you have to check these things about twice a day during the calving season."

Across the road from the Erickson ranch, you can see the magnitude of repair that's required where the soil is less stable or the job is less promptly begun. A year ago there was a large, growing canyon here, twenty-five feet deep in spots, gnawing its way up to a gentle summit between hills. Now a small army of workers is reshaping the entire landscape: replacing the vertical, crumbling sides with gently sloped embankments; regrading the drainage bottom with low, sediment-trapping berms; lining the channel with protective "geotextile fabric" and seeding adjacent ground to grass. When the work is done, the whole area will be fenced to keep stock out for a number of years.

Lee Erickson, one of Leroy's sons and in effect a partner on the ranch, has more than a neighborly interest in the goings-on across the road. As a consulting engineer to the Gold Ridge Resource Conservation District, he is helping in an ambitious state-funded attack on erosion in the Estero Americano watershed. It was Lee, in fact, who helped the nearby landowner make arrangements, surveyed and designed the project, and steered it through its government approvals. He's done it all many times.

The Ericksons now graze more animals per acre than they used to. They've achieved that capacity gradually, building up the range through seeding and fertilization. "There's no sign of overgrazing," Leroy says with matter-of-fact pride. They watch the situation carefully, though. "In ranching," Agnes notes, "what works today may not work tomorrow. We're always adjusting our practices. All ranchers do."

One of their range-improvement weapons is the ingenious burr clover, a nutritious annual legume with seeds in small soft burrs. These pass undigested through cows and sheep and then lie dormant, encased in fertilizing dung, until the autumn rains come. To get the clover established on their ranch, the Ericksons planted it one season in their hayfield, fed the hay to their stock, and let nature do the rest. "We've got it just about everywhere, now." Leroy dissects a cowflop with his boot to show the first paired leaves.

"It would have been interesting to see this area three or four hundred years ago, wouldn't it?" asks Leroy Erickson. "To see what the hills and the valleys looked like? These valleys probably had live streams in them most of the year, little trickling streams, before they were silted in."

The Ericksons can't put the land back to what it was in Miwok times. They can't undo what happened in less knowledgeable days. But they can make sure that soil erosion goes no farther; they can even begin to restore what has been lost. "The way I look at it," says Leroy Erickson, "we don't really own the land. We're here for a short period of time. Stewards, that's what we really are."

Five   ■   THE LAND IN TRUST

It was a little embarrassing. After the excitement and publicity of its 1980 founding, the new Marin Agricultural Land Trust seemed, for a while, almost to disappear. MALT was there, of course, and working hard; but nobody had quite reckoned with the number of quiet preliminary jobs to be done before a single acre of actual farmland could be labeled "saved."

The new organization had to design itself and the legal instruments it would use. It had a long way to go toward gaining the confidence of the ranching community. And it had to raise serious money.

In earlier days the county itself would have contributed heavily, but in 1978 the voters had passed tax-slashing Proposition 13; any such expenditure would now require a nearly prohibitive two-thirds yes-vote at the polls. The supervisors did allocate to the trust one-tenth of a shrunken stream of money reserved for purchases of open space: an important sign of support, but nickels and dimes in terms of the job to be done.

The gap was filled, in large part, by the Leonard and Beryl Buck trust, an enormous fund dedicated specifically to Marin County projects and administered, at the time, by the San Francisco Foundation. The foundation made a practice of helping the Marin Agricultural Land Trust with its overhead and soon added a project grant of $200,000. (The Marin Community Foundation, which took over management of the Buck bequest in 1986, would continue this habit of support.)

Marin's experiment, meanwhile, was attracting more than local interest. Seeing that lessons learned here might be applicable elsewhere, the state's Coastal Conservancy stepped in, contributing $317,000 in 1982 and in

Cypresses along an old ranch road

1984, a full $1,000,000. The latter grant was contingent on a match from the Buck fund. After some suspense, that source again came through.

By this time MALT had a respectable war chest and was open for business. Interested customers appeared—at first one or two bold ones, then more, then many.

The first property MALT preserved was the 844-acre Mazza-Pomi ranch in northern Marin near Petaluma. The payment made for the development rights enabled a third-generation ranching family to stay on land it had considered selling. Then came Maggetti, Skywalker, Walker Creek, LaFranchi, Hick's Valley, Cerini, Tamagno, Barboni, Parker, Spaletta. . . . By 1989, the land trust had acquired development rights on more than 11,500 acres. There were protected ranches, a whole cluster of them, near the village of Nicasio, an area threatened by parcel breakup; a string of properties along the Marshall–Petaluma Road, part lofty ridge line and part hidden canyon; several sloping chunks along Tomales Bay; a strategic piece on the outskirts of Tomales town. Perhaps the most spectacular and threatened of them all was a windswept ranch at the far northwestern corner of the county, now safely under easement and owned by Jim Spaletta; it borders both the ocean and the Estero Americano, the fragile estuary that here forms the county line.

The trust, an unknown quantity at first, is now a reassuring presence even to ranchers who don't currently wish to sell their A-60 rights. They know it's there, an option, a resource. Operations that are just humming along may not consider MALT; operations that face changes—an operator's retirement, for instance— are more likely to.

A Fighting Chance

In June 1988, California voters passed, by a margin of almost two to one, a huge bond issue for parks, wildlife habitat, and farmland preservation, Proposition 70. Included for conservation easements in Marin: $15 million over ten years.

Technically, MALT does not buy development rights; it acquires *agricultural land conservation easements,* which prohibit "residential or commercial development and uses or practices which would be destructive to the agricultural value and productivity of the land." Legally, the distinction is quite necessary. In commonsense terms, it matters not at all.

In most cases MALT has paid for easements, but outright gifts, too, have been substantial. They show how useful a trust can be simply as a reliable recipient. The San Francisco Foundation, for instance, once purchased several West Marin properties; it disposed of them variously but gave almost all the development rights to MALT. In another case, when the county allowed filmmaker George Lucas to build a studio on what is now Skywalker ranch near Nicasio, it more or less required him to donate the A-60 development rights to MALT. Other such windfalls will probably occur.

When, by contrast, MALT pays for the rights, it is helping local agriculture in two ways at once: by protecting land and by injecting money. Development potential always was a one-time cash crop; now a farmer can harvest it without also losing the land. The proceeds of that harvest may be used to stabilize an operation in trouble; to expand a thriving one; to buy land or stock or equipment; to pay off a mortgage; to build a retirement fund; to assist a land transfer between generations; or perhaps to buy out a co-owner who isn't interested in agriculture.

The price MALT pays for easements has ranged from about one-quarter to about one-half of the unrestricted value of the land. In dollar terms the range, during the 1980s, was from under $300 to nearly $1,000 per acre. Future costs, boosted by inflation and climbing land values, will certainly be much higher. The transactions have

How far will $15 million go? There are, outside the parks, some 145,000 acres in Marin's agricultural belt. Almost 12,000 acres are already secured; MALT estimates that the new state money could buy rights on between 25,000 and 35,000 acres more. In sight, then, is a remarkable goal: protection, by easement, of one-third of a county's entire stock of agricultural land.

And what then? If every rancher in the county eventually decided to sell rights to MALT, the total cost—at today's prices, in today's dollars—could top $100 million. That's comparable to the amount the federal government has spent to acquire its vast Marin County parks. Whether that kind of money can be raised is an open question. Perhaps gifts and skillful use of development-rights *transfers* will allow the job to be done for less. It is possible, too, that some part of the job will never require doing. Maybe MALT will stabilize local agriculture as much by its very existence, by its quiet availability, as it does through its actual transactions. Maybe its success will be measured someday by the amount of land it did not touch, there being no threat, no need.

But it is far too soon to count on successes either subtle or overt. MALT and the county's policies have given agriculture a fighting chance, no more. The future is a long way from secure.

Periodically, the dairy business goes through hard times. Each episode forces a few ranchers out of business. A few people enter the business, as well, but never quite as many as depart; the list of active dairies continues to get shorter. In 1989, Marin had just fifty-two.

Pollution control is again becoming a challenge. Since the mid-1970s, when the first waste management systems went in, many ranchers have increased their herds; wastewater ponds and irrigation setups now need expansion to match. The pollution control authorities, meanwhile, are looking for means to further protect the waters of Tomales Bay.

Land prices in western Marin are still dauntingly high—for the farmer. For the urban refugee, the would-be hobby farmer who can cash in property "over the hill" for a truly fantastic sum, they don't seem high at all: so he tends to bid them higher. Even properties devoid of development rights may now sell for amounts greater than ranchers can afford. There is real fear today of what might be called "mega-ranchettes": recreational farms not of sixty acres

Black Mountain behind Point Reyes Station

taken various forms. In one common pattern, MALT teams up with a rancher who's in the market for land. MALT buys the development rights on a parcel; the rancher pays the rest of the asking price and becomes the owner.

In most cases, the development rights acquired with ease-ments have simply been wiped off the books. MALT has yet to make use of the logical exten-sion, transfer of development rights, in which the rights are actually exercised—but in places where agriculture is not harmed. The trust now holds a number of such rights that it could sell for this use. If MALT begins to sell as well as to buy, it will acquire a revolving fund, and its money should go some-what farther.

The trick in TDR, of course, is finding the right spot for the added building. It is a given that development is limited to that permitted in the Marin Countywide Plan. There are a few spots where the plan would allow more development than is permitted by existing zoning, and these are places where the rights held by MALT might conceivably be used.

Two of the likeliest sites are the Nicasio Valley and the village of Marshall on the eastern shore of Tomales Bay. In these places county ordinances and adopted community plans encourage farmland preservation by offering would-be developers a special option: they can increase density on nonagricultural building sites by purchasing additional development rights from agricultural land. The one transaction that has actually taken place, the LaFranchi transfer near Nicasio, has not involved MALT; but future developers may well be purchasing rights from the MALT-owned pool.

but of four hundred or five or even six hundred acres. Such vast rural estates might not clutter the landscape as the small ones do, but they would weaken agriculture in some of the same ways.

MALT is now studying ways of keeping the price of easement-restricted land within a range that farmers can afford. For instance, rather than acquiring development rights alone, MALT might also acquire a part interest in the properties themselves. Such a program would require a good deal more money than development-rights purchase by itself.

Someday, conceivably, *all* development rights may be gone from West Marin ranches; unless and until that day comes, it is a working, sustainable, profit-making agriculture that keeps the countryside intact.

And what if that day should come? What if, in a decade or two or three, development is so nearly precluded that the open character of the landscape no longer directly depends on the industry that occupies it?

It is possible to imagine a West Marin given over to semi-wild estates, horse ranches, parks, institutional properties, and the like—a sleek green landscape, rural certainly, as good to look at as ever, but no longer, not fundamentally, agricultural. To the conservationists of 1970, such an outcome might have seemed a very good deal. Even today, some people might cheerfully say, Let agriculture go. That chorus would be small, however. Marin's attitude toward its farms has changed fundamentally since the early 1970s.

Something vital and gritty and engaging would be lost to the county and the region if the ranching culture died. That was always so. Now it is recognized.

The Three Giacominis
(Point Reyes Station, San Rafael)

Somehow the name Giacomini never stays out of the news in West Marin for long. One fellow so surnamed is the county supervisor who represents the region. A second sits on the Marin Agricultural Land Trust board. A third is the owner of a piece of ground that—so it seems—is permanently controversial.

The Waldo Giacomini ranch, just outside Point Reyes Station, is like no other in this countryside. It's flat. It's low. And more than anything else, it's green. The water that keeps it that way year-round comes from Papermill or Lagunitas Creek, the county's largest stream, which empties here into the head of Tomales Bay. Places where fresh and salt water come together tend to be crossroads, ecological, commercial, and political: so here.

In the days of the West Marin General Plan, the Giacomini ranch was meant for a busy future. Much of it was going to be a massive shopping center, most of the rest, a "lagoon residential" complex. This spot was going to be the hub of West Marin. If Waldo Giacomini looked forward to prosperous days, he could scarcely be blamed.

Meanwhile, the rancher sought to add to his working acreage by diking off some tidelands he owned in the bay. Ten years earlier, such an action would have bothered no one; but by 1970 wetland preservation was a Cause. Marin conservationists turned out a navy of small boats and canoes and staged a floating demonstration in the threatened shallows. The county turned down the fill request, and a few months later Giacomini sold his tide flats to the state for a wildlife refuge. "I don't like to fight," he told the *Point Reyes Light*. "It's best to go along with the times."

A TALE OF TWO COUNTIES

Marin ranchers look north in some suspense to Sonoma County, the neighboring jurisdiction that contains two-thirds of the North Bay dairy belt and, in the town of Petaluma, its principal service center. Tight though the links across the boundary are (with many families ranching on both sides) the political lessons of Marin's experiment in land preservation have made no easy crossing. Sonoma County has had to work out its own solutions from scratch. The emerging results have much in common with Marin policies—but with a lag of a decade or more.

It was in fact in 1985, against strong opposition, that the Sonoma Board of Supervisors first imposed large-parcel zoning in the dairy belt (zoning analogous to, and on paper a bit stronger than, A-60). There is still some doubt as to how well it will stick. As in Marin after 1972, this is a testing time.

The surrounding debate has been full of the old confusions. Are strong land-use

But the times had only started changing. Soon they had carried off the West Marin General Plan. In 1972, A-60 zoning began. The Giacomini ranch was in one of the first batches of land to be reclassified. At the crucial meeting of the Board of Supervisors, a young candidate for supervisor spoke up to endorse the zoning: Gary Giacomini.

The two Giacominis were not, in fact, very closely related, by blood or background. They share only a great-grandfather, and Gary Giacomini's side of the family had been in town for years; his father was county clerk during the 1950s. He loved the rural scene, but the way an urban conservationist is likely to love it: as a *scene.*

Gary Giacomini remembers that meeting well. "The room was packed. All these lawyers and everybody. And little Gary gets up and says, 'I think A-60 is the way to go.' With which, every rancher in the county thinks, 'We know who our enemy is.'

"They thought I was some freak from over the hills, some wacko guy that was going to zone them to the Stone Age. Make them provide the open space that urban people wanted, so we all could drive by and say, 'Oh, look, there's a black and white cow.'

"See it from their point of view. You've done this for three or four generations, and you're working too hard and your fences are falling down and, what the hell, there's probably enough milk anyway. And some kid politician comes along and tells you, 'You've got to do this forever. Whether you like it or not.'

"They thought I didn't understand, and they were right. I didn't understand the agonies of the day-to-day life. I didn't understand the families, how it is they get by."

That began to change for Gary Giacomini when he got into office. It changed still faster when he spent several years living on the Straus ranch. "I remember when Bill was going to send this little calf to auction, and I said, 'No, no'—and I took it on and I nursed it with a bottle and all . . . but over the years I found out what the life was like, and I realized: you couldn't just zone these people into oblivion and walk away."

All through the rest of the decade—through the pollution control crisis, the drought emergency, the pivotal milk-price hearings, the first stirrings toward a Marin Agricultural Land Trust—Giacomini's relation to the farm belt

"It's not that we're smarter here. It could be that we're luckier." Supervisor Gary Giacomini trying his luck on Western Weekend.

kept shifting. Largely because of his advocacy, the county "began to put its money where its zoning mouth was." In the 1976 election, a few of his relatives supported him. In later elections, virtually all of them did.

"I'd have guys come up to me and shake my hand and say kind of gruffly, 'Well, you son of a bitch, you weren't just trying to screw us, after all.'"

Among other improbable things, Gary has found himself defending his distant cousin, Waldo, from the attacks of one faction among the environmentalists. Some people sincerely feel that the mouth of Papermill Creek is a spot of such importance in the natural scheme that it should be taken out of agriculture and made a wildlife sanctuary, now. Failing that, they keep a jealous eye on what goes on there, watching for any practice that might conceivably harm the stream, the fish for which it is a major habitat and highway, and the bay it feeds. One sign of how greatly things have changed is that so many among the county's conservationists line up these days—after a look at the ecological details—on Waldo Giacomini's side.

"It's a complicated world out there. Much more so than I thought when I was a kid." So says Robert Giacomini, whose ranch on Bolinas Ridge just

controls pro-agriculture or anti-agriculture? Don't farmers need the ability to sell off building sites in order to survive? Isn't dairy ranching doomed, anyway? Who could make a living that way? Sonomans seem reluctant, almost in a patriotic sense, to take into account the experience of Marin.

Looking south across the invisible boundary near Two Rock, Sonoma dairyman Paul Martin sees another world. The fundamental fact, says Martin, is simply that in Marin the commitment to the dairy belt is taken seriously; in Sonoma, he worries, it will prove mere pos-

turing. The Sonoma supervisors, he feels, are "far too willing to subordinate farmland to urban domestic needs." For instance, a current search for a new county dump site seems to be zeroing in on ranch properties.

And he recalls seeing a ranch near Petaluma advertised for sale in the *Wall Street Journal*. The land, under Williamson Act contract, was zoned for agriculture. At the bottom of the ad, in fine print, appeared the words: "Zoning available." He's afraid that, ultimately, that will prove to be the case.

north of Point Reyes Station overlooks the briskly shifting waters of Tomales Bay and, some distance south, the verdant Point Reyes Station property of his father, Waldo.

The two ranches could hardly be more different. This acreage is dry, sky-open, westward-tilted. Climbing its slope on a long paved driveway, you don't at first see the dairy buildings at all. They are hidden down in a draw. "They built that way before they had pumps," Robert says, "to be downhill from the springs"—and out of the wind whose organizing force keeps the trees, too, confined to the low spots. The very modern house, by contrast, is westward on a knoll, where the view is wide and the flies absent.

Giacomini has reacted to the complications of his business a little more aggressively than some. Since he started here in 1960, he has built his herd up from 130 to 500 cows—one of the county's largest. Back in 1967, when so massive an investment was unusual, he built a free-stall barn to keep his animals out of the winter mud. "I was a little too energetic, I guess." A few years later, in the cause of pollution control, the county might have footed part of the bill.

We're talking now in his office, a sort of indoor balcony overhanging the busy milking floor. So automated is the operation that one employee—he has seven in all—can control a milking of his half a thousand cows. His newest installation is a computerized system that tells him instantly, even as the milking progresses, how much each animal is yielding and how long it is taking to milk her. Out in the yard, the waiting animals are nudged along gently by a rolling fence. At intervals, powerful sprinklers set in the pavement come on, making sure that udders are clean.

Obviously, Bob Giacomini is settling in for the long haul. "I have hope for the dairy industry in Marin, or else I would have signed up for the whole herd buyout program . . . I think it's going to work out for the good operators." He is a director of the Marin Agricultural Land Trust, but he doubts that the trust can purchase easements quickly enough or on a scale large enough to protect the farm belt if the dairy business falters. "If the dairymen cannot survive in this county, development will happen. The pressures will be too great."

How about the surplus problem? "That's one of the complicated issues." Giacomini doesn't want to see American farmers adopt rigid production quotas like the ones in Canada or Europe, but he notes: "If every dairy in the United States eliminated one cow, the problem would disappear." One of his opinions is highly unusual for a rancher: he would welcome some kind of national zoning to protect land for agriculture (and to mark other land for appropriate development).

If Marin does go under, there's always the Central Valley, isn't there? Not for Robert Giacomini. "I wouldn't go to the Valley to dairy. Even if I could double my income. I don't like the climate, period. The cows don't like it much, either."

The Commissioner: Jerry Friedman (Point Reyes Station)

Marin County Counsel Douglas Maloney had a problem. After years without a challenge, A-60 zoning was under legal attack. Maloney had to retrace in

If Martin is wrong—if the Sonoma policies succeed—he himself can take some of the credit (as a tireless and often lonely advocate of farmland preservation through "agricultural production zones").

The major engine of change in Sonoma County has been the very effective Sonoma County Farmlands Group, established in 1980. It reflects an alliance of environmentalists and agriculturalists somewhat like the one in Marin County, but with one key difference. In Sonoma, it is the grape growers and the wine makers, not yet the dairymen and livestock raisers, who have come to see their interest in defending agricultural land.

Marin ranchers have a more than neighborly interest in the struggle next door. If the Sonoma dairies go under, Marin dairymen fear, the Marin County fragment of the belt would be too small to go it alone. Should the agricultural support industries start leaving Petaluma, the end would be near.

court the reasoning the county had gone through when it adopted the rigorous zone—and show the notes and documents produced along the way.

The almost incredible hitch: nowhere—not in Planning Department files, not in Board of Supervisors minutes, not in cardboard boxes rumored to be "downstairs"—could he lay hands on these historic and suddenly vital pieces of paper.

Maloney put out a call to everyone he could think of who'd had a part in that decision. The one response he got, from former Planning Commissioner Jerry Friedman of Point Reyes Station, was the only one he needed. A triumphant packrat, Friedman had kept the papers that others had thrown away. When others had made mental notes, he had made notes in ink. When others had lost their files, his were found.

Jerry Friedman had started the decade of the 1970s as an activist, cofounder of the Environmental Action Committee of West Marin, no special friend of the ranchers in their eyes or his own. In 1973, to some apprehension in the farm belt, Gary Giacomini appointed him to a seat on the Planning Commission.

Almost the first case that came before the new commissioner was a challenge to agricultural zoning. On the Point Reyes–Petaluma Road, opposite the Marin French Cheese Factory, a sprawling residential development was proposed. The commission killed it by a vote of six to one. The developer, as is usual with important cases, appealed to the Board of Supervisors.

"It was crucial," Friedman recalls. "If we'd started backing away then, there'd have been no stopping." He remembers pleading with one wavering supervisor. "I'm afraid we'll wind up in court," the supervisor complained. "Maybe we should," Friedman replied. But that time, when the supervisors denied the appeal, no suit was filed.

What struck Friedman about this controversy, though, was what some local ranchers said. These landowners—no supporters of the zoning when imposed—now came forward to defend it. (In later years, ranchers would even petition the commission for *additional* A-60 zoning on lands that had been skipped.)

In those first years on the commission, Friedman developed a particular style. Though a man of strong opinions, he learned to wait, to hear all sides, to listen. "I pride myself on never knowing how I'm going to vote." He got to noticing a difference between liberals and conservatives, including ranchers. "The Left dumped on me any time I didn't do what they wanted. The Right was so happy that I listened to them before I voted, and that I occasionally would side with them, that they befriended me."

Then came the 1976–1977 drought. "That opened a door." With others, Friedman formed a Committee for Family Farms to support the ranchers during the emergency, especially in their request for a temporary milk-price increase to offset the cost of hauling water and the lofty price of hay. At one of the Sacramento milk-price hearings he received, "from two or three hundred red-necks, the most astonishing ovation I've ever gotten for anything."

And so he learned, by doing it, how environmentalists can build an alliance with farmers. "It isn't enough to support them in general," he says. "You've got to show them that you'll fight for them when you can." That doesn't mean automatic support: "You find and pick issues where you *can* help them."

In 1980, one Richard M. Barancik, a Chicago architect, bought a hilltop ranch on the big bald peak called Loma Alta, a county landmark near the edge of the urban strip. Loma Alta had long been zoned A-60, allowing only nine homesites there, but Barancik wanted more: twenty-eight "luxury ranch-ettes." After the inevitable turndown by the county, Barancik went to court, arguing that county zoning prevented "any economically meaningful private use of the property" and that it was not evenhandedly applied. It was then, in 1985, that Maloney issued his call for historical paperwork.

Meanwhile, in 1983, Jerry Friedman had left the Planning Commission. "I was burned out. I knew what everybody was going to say—I could finish their sentences for them. And I'd get too emotionally involved." But he kept on working with farm issues: as a director of the Marin Agricultural Land Trust, and as chair of the Point Reyes committee of a body called the Golden Gate National Recreation Area Citizens' Advisory Commission. In this job, he supervised the preparation of new and tougher grazing regulations for ranches in Point Reyes National Seashore. On the side, he functioned as a sort of trouble-shooter when problems came up between ranchers and environmentalists.

In 1989, after losing a succession of decisions and appeals, Barancik got the final resounding No: the United States Supreme Court declined to review the matter further.

It was also in 1989 that Friedman, accepting a standing invitation, went back on the Planning Commission. "I kept thinking of issues that I cared about. And believe me, it isn't that I know where I stand on them!"

He's taking notes.

The Teacher Goes to School: Phyllis Faber (Mill Valley)

The friendship between Marin County ranchers and conservationists—now seen as a basic fact of life—didn't just happen. It might never have happened. It was started and sustained by *individuals:* a few key people on either side who were willing to abandon the old script of hostility and start improvising dialogue of their own.

How were they able to do it? Along with natural flexibility of mind, it seems to have required education—some routine contact with the other side, and some familiarity with the world as those others saw it.

Take Phyllis Faber, biologist, New York City–bred. But from her father, a transplanted Californian who had spent time on a sheep ranch near Cloverdale, she got a vivid if secondhand impression of life on the rural land. It stuck. "I really have that as a heritage," she says. "I always look at land, at what it grows."

Faber looks also at water and what water grows. The destruction of wetlands—marshes and riparian habitats—was the first conservation issue to catch her imagination. (She has published two field guides on the subject.) In the late 1960s, she plunged into the campaign for a California coastal protection law. After the voters passed such a law in 1972, Faber was appointed to the North Central Regional Coastal Commission.

It was also in 1972 that she helped to found the Environmental Forum of Marin, a sort of floating college for local citizens that offers dozens of courses a year on natural history, environmental issues, and planning questions. Its campus is the whole county; its students tend to be youngish adults headed for leadership positions in government and elsewhere. A Marin *Who's Who* would be rich in the forum's graduates. ("The San Francisco Foundation once turned us down for a grant on the grounds that we didn't influence enough people. I thought that was pretty amazing.")

In both roles—as an Environmental Forum instructor, as a coastal commissioner—Faber started visiting coastal farms.

At first, local ranchers faced the Coastal Commission, and Faber, with trepidation. "A female from East Marin and on the commission was pretty spooky." But, she goes on, "the ranchers soon realized that we would never stand in the way of putting up a barn, things like that . . . though they didn't like government, I think they were impressed that a lot of farmland that had gone out of use along the coast came back in because of the coastal law."

The major Marin case that Faber faced during those years was a proposed tourist lodge near Marshall. By turning down the proposal—"we just couldn't say yes. The Coastal Act guidelines didn't permit it"— the commission essentially forced a revision in the Marin Countywide Plan. Where the plan had looked for a mix of ranching and resort development along the shore (a compound of doubtful stability), the commission insisted that agriculture be put first.

In the course of this work, Faber saw farms that were well managed and some that were not; she had a chance to compare properties run by their owners with others occupied by tenants. She became skeptical of plans to save the rural landscape by buying land outright and leasing it back to farmers. "It's inescapable," she says. "Land managed by the owner is better off." She also became aware of how fragile a land-preservation tool local government zoning typically is—and how vulnerable to political pressures even the Coastal Commission could be.

Meanwhile, back at the forum, she and Ellen Straus, the noted rancher and conservationist from Marshall, had become friends. In 1978, the two conducted a special minicourse on farm issues, with visits to eight local ranches; this led to the first of many Family Farm Day tours.

And one afternoon's farm visit led to more than that. "We'd had sort of a yeasty discussion at Boyd Stewart's place. He started us thinking about the long-term fate of agriculture in the county and I think that's when Ellen and I decided that if something could be done, it should be done."

That something turned out to be the Marin Agricultural Land Trust. She has served from the beginning on its rancher-dominated board; in 1989, she was elected president.

Faber's Coastal Commission career ended in 1979 (shortly before the regional commissions were dissolved). Her Environmental Forum work goes on. She estimates that she has personally brought more than two thousand people out to the ranches of West Marin. "We really need to keep people in East Marin aware of the farms, to keep the decisions at the Civic Center supportive of agriculture."

How does Faber feel when—as occasionally happens—two of her prime commitments, to agriculture and to wetlands, come into conflict? "Sometimes," she admits, "I'm sliced down the middle. If I had to make a really hard choice, I probably would wind up on the side of the wetlands." But, she points out, many conflicts are less serious than they seem. Diked fields, for instance, flood in winter and make good habitat for wetland-dependent birds.

The City Stops Here:
George and Annette Grossi (Novato)

Even today some ranchers live quite isolated lives. A few remote farmsteads didn't get gas and electric power till the 1960s, and one visitor to a ranch far out on Point Reyes exclaimed: "This has to be the last place God created. He couldn't go any farther."

At the other extreme are those farms that lie right on the urban fringe, where the crossroads store might be a 7-Eleven. If the city next door is spreading outward, ready to overwhelm the rural fringe, that's a disconcerting place to live, tugged at by the natural hope of real estate profit and the equally natural sadness at the prospective loss of land that (count on it!) has been loved.

But if a ranch family lives on a *fixed* urban fringe—where city and country have a treaty of peace, so to speak, establishing a long-term boundary—that's different. Says Annette Grossi, who lives with her husband, George, and three kids on the western edge of Novato, at the gateway to West Marin: "It's the best of both the worlds."

*George Grossi and Farm Bureau friends
at the Family Farm Day barbecue*

*"We've lost a lot of dairies in Marin,"
George Grossi tells a Family Farm Day
crowd. "We haven't lost a lot of cows."
Annette Grossi (right).*

George Grossi was born on this ranch in 1948. In 1953 his father sold one
hundred acres to the North Marin Water District for construction of Stafford
Lake reservoir, Novato's chief water supply. In the late 1960s, the neighborhood of San Marin went up on former dairy land a couple of miles away. In
1971, a second chunk of the Grossi ranch went to the county for a park. Urban
neighbors, urban water supply, urban playground: the Grossis are right there.

And lately, during commute hours, they have found themselves facing urban traffic as well: desperate auto commuters, trying to avoid the jams on Highway 101, have learned that it saves them time to make a dogleg into West Marin, right past the Grossis' front fence.

George and Annette moved onto the ranch just as the county was wedging shut the door, till then wide open, to the urbanization of all West Marin. The Grossis scarcely noticed the change. Since their remaining 420 acres lie in the sensitive Stafford Lake watershed, they'd already made their adjustment to the thought of staying where they were—and liking it.

Living on the fringe, they get to pick and choose. "In thirty minutes we can be in San Francisco," says Annette. "We can go to art shows, to museums, to performances. And some of our best friends live over in town." But daughter Rachel—like her brother, sister, and father before her—attends a one-room school, Lincoln, out on Hick's Valley Road. The kids' free time may be split between 4H projects and summer sports teams run by Novato Park and Rec.

George's connections run toward the rural community; he faces west. He serves on the Lincoln School District board. He heads the local Dairy Herd Improvement Association. He chairs the important Land Use Committee of the Farm Bureau and in 1988 became a director of the Marin Agricultural Land Trust. This puts him in the middle of what has been called The Incredible Coalition: the alliance of urban and rural interests that has succeeded, so far, in shielding Marin agriculture from development pressures on the one hand and, on the other, from environmental controls too abruptly or too uncomprehendingly applied. Grossi finds most environmentalists "exceptionally good people to work with." His wife agrees: "The city people in their suits are mostly pretty sympathetic. There shouldn't be cross-purposes, and usually there aren't."

All this activity means *meetings*—some seemingly indispensable gathering about every other evening. Then there's the basic ranch work, unrelenting here as anywhere. George's day runs from 5:30 in the morning until midnight—later, if there's a crisis in the barn.

Annette is equally busy, but her work lies east. For fifteen years, even while raising a family, she's been a sort of roving ambassador and missionary to the urban community, especially to town-raised kids. It worries her how little these urban youngsters know of the systems that sustain them. "Agriculture is your basis for living. A lot of people forget that."

But they don't if Annette Grossi is around. She pushed the idea of the annual Farm Day at the county's Civic Center (an event distinct from the Family Farm Day tour) and chairs the committee that keeps it going. She lobbied to have commercial agriculture represented at the county fair; now, along with backyard tomatoes, there's a lively farm and ranch section, where visitors can see and sometimes touch those once-familiar creatures that, to many of us, have become as exotic as the inmates of zoos: sheep and cows, goats and rabbits, hogs and chickens and geese—along with that newcomer to local agriculture, the useful and personable llama (when it's mad at you, it *hums*). Teacher training, poster and mural contests, classroom appearances: the Grossi list goes on.

At the center of the work, though, has been the hectic two-month period in spring when the Grossi ranch is opened to tours from public schools. As many as two thousand children and adults, drawn from Marin, Sonoma, San Francisco, and the East Bay, have tramped through milk barn and hay barn in a single season. On occasion, Lesha, Dominic, and Rachel have done the guiding ("kids sometimes respond better to kids").

As we talk, Lesha is making a shopping list. "You don't have to buy soap," George jokes. "You can take lard from the pigs we butcher and boil it down." "Oh, Dad," says Lesha.

"All in all," says Annette, "I think we're making a dent."

Youngsters from this part of Marin County don't go next door to Novato for junior high and high school. Instead, they take a bus ride west and north across the county line to Petaluma. One sign of the reason why: Petaluma High School has a department of agriculture. Petaluma is by long tradition the capital of the Marin-Sonoma dairy belt.

But if the Marin dairy community looks north, it isn't always comforted by what it sees. As Sonoma County gains population, its people, too, are losing the old connections to the land. "Kids up in Rohnert Park," says Annette, "are as unknowledgeable about agriculture as the San Francisco ones." And Sonoma has yet to achieve the consensus about farmland that Marin has had for fifteen years.

Six ▪ MARIN THE MODEL?

"It's sure not that we're smarter here," Supervisor Gary Giacomini has remarked. "It may be that we're luckier." Indeed, it seems sometimes as though some minor agricultural deity has been keeping an eye on West Marin's green hills.

Part of the luck was in the hills themselves: through the dangerous years after World War II when no mere government rules could have set limits to horizontal growth, the terrain kept development confined to the eastern corridor. By the time westward pressure began to mount, planners had more tools.

The county was lucky again that the beauty of its coastline, so close to a metropolitan center, drew the federal government to buy vast tracts for parks. In 1962, when Point Reyes National Seashore was authorized, no lesser force could possibly have kept the coastlands intact. Even in 1972, when the Golden Gate National Recreation Area was created, the future of the Olema Valley ranches it encompassed was in some doubt.

It was helpful, too, that Marin's farmers haven't felt the same economic squeeze as their colleagues in, say, Iowa. Local agriculture doesn't run extensively on debt, so the punishing interest rates of the early 1980s were not disastrous to it.

More? How about the almost outrageous Beryl Buck inheritance. In 1978, a wealthy and generous woman left a bequest to the people of Marin County: some ten million dollars' worth of stock in a minor oil company, the income to be used for good works in this county alone. By 1986, the value of the trust had exploded to $400 million. Several million dollars of the interest from that vast principal have gone directly or indirectly to the farmland protection cause.

In 1980, even as MALT was being founded in Point Reyes Station, a national organization devoted specifically to farmland preservation was forming in Washington, D.C.: the American Farmland Trust (AFT). In 1986, the trust lured Marin dairyman Ralph Grossi away from his ranch on Novato Boulevard to become AFT's executive director. Marin's experience had been noticed; and Grossi's selection made it certain that it would be noticed further. "Marin is the model," Grossi said.

But is it? Can a case so special be a model for anyone?

It depends on what's meant by *model.* If a model is something you copy, Marin's achievement doesn't qualify: few other places could borrow its methods intact. If a model is something you look at and learn from, the label fits.

And in one respect, at least, this county had a harder than usual job to do in safeguarding agricultural land. Here the resource in question was not farmland as we usually conceive it: not deep-soiled cropland, brimming with edibles. Instead, it was grazing country, handsome but rather bony-looking. West Marin would have been unaffected, for example, by statewide zoning aimed at preserving "prime agricultural land," as discussed in the state legislature in the early 1970s. And there was no way the Marin County rancher, even the dairy rancher, could outbid a potential developer in an open-market competition for land. If that is true for most types of agriculture, it is doubly true for "mere" grazing land.

What Marin did, in short, should be somewhat easier to do in regions where the economic value of farmland as farmland is higher.

Can the Last Places Last?

Back when the Marin Countywide Plan was appearing, one of its satellites was an environmental study entitled *Can the Last Place Last?* The question became a slogan, a motif. Appealing to the always-ready local patriotism, it also touched a larger reality. Places like this county, where farmlands and wildlands remain in strange proximity to swelling urban centers, all have that threatened, treasurable quality. They are, all, last places.

What does this one very local experiment have to teach about the means of preserving other such landscapes, other such countrysides?

The quick and almost banal lesson might be: if you plan to preserve some agricultural land, hold nothing back. Use every tool, every idea that comes to hand. But more can be said than that.

In first place stands a truth that many within the county, in these days of good feeling, prefer not to emphasize. Simply put: The government's No to development in farm areas must come before—at least not after—the government's Yes to farmers' other needs. Within the chosen boundaries, regulators must absolutely and consistently refuse to permit incompatible development. Such action will often mean, as it did in Marin, imposing unpopular, arguably hurtful, rules. But had this not been done, none of the rest—the rescue efforts on pollution control and in the drought, the formation of an urban-rural alliance, the founding and swift progress of MALT—could have come after. Support without land use controls would have been wasted money.

If local governments can't draw firm lines, other powers may be called on to do so. In California and many other states, an aroused local public can take the controls itself. This has in fact occurred in two Bay Area counties, Solano and San Mateo: by direct initiative, the voters of these counties have overruled their boards of supervisors and curtailed development outside city boundaries. In other cases, special regional or state agencies can be set up to do the job, either by a legislature or, again, by the voters themselves (as when Californians first created the Coastal Commissions).

Will such regulations stand up in court? If they are carefully designed, if they are consistently enforced, they will. The final 1989 decision in the Barancik case was the latest in the long series of court rulings affirming that.

The second major lesson is more kindly. The Marin case suggests that the mere exercise of power, in the spirit, There are more of us than there are of you, may not be enough. A government wanting to help agriculture compete against urbanization needs also to find ways of helping the land-based industry.

Dolcini home ranch in Hick's Valley

Couldn't the job be done by regulation alone? Perhaps in some places it could. In Marin, where an early collapse of the dairy industry could have undermined the basic regulation, land-use controls without further support might have been ultimately futile. It seems safe to say that an approach aiming toward consensus, the consent of the regulated, will have more durable results than one that never gets beyond restrictive rules.

The trick is to maintain a clear distinction between the interests of landowning farmers as speculators (and what landowner is not at least aware of it when values climb?) and the different interests of those same people as farm operators. After using every power to frustrate the farmer-as-speculator, Marin County worked just as hard to make life easier for the farmer-as-farmer. That's the key.

Of all the things that happened in Marin, the one most noted elsewhere was the building of a three-way coalition: the coming together of ranchers with conservationists and with leaders in the local government. It isn't easy to do by plan what evolved, in this one spot, over years of conflict and adjustment, but various localities are trying.

Marin's experience suggests that such coalitions won't be a matter of organization charts. They will depend on a few key individuals: farmers deeply committed to farming, environmentalists who seek out issues on which they can offer farmers support, and one or more key political figures who take on what might be called the agriculture portfolio. The Marin policy revolution began before the arrival of Supervisor Gary Giacomini, yet it is Giacomini who is usually credited with keeping it on course for the following eighteen years.

Who makes the first move toward coalition? In Marin, the government and the environmental side led off, and perhaps this will be generally true. At first such contacts may be stiff and difficult, a mere exchange of views; with luck and work, they may lead to genuine good feeling; at the very least, the people involved will shed some prejudices and learn which of the issues that divide them can be compromised and which cannot.

When Marin County set out to preserve its agriculture, it was frankly as a means to another end. Farmland was open space, a framework to limit, shape, and beautify the urban growth enclosed within it. As time went on, the talk shifted to the value of the farms themselves. Although the two approaches are not at all in conflict—each implies the other—this attitude shift may be essential to the job of preserving agricultural open space. Certainly you don't get far with farmers if you don't learn to see the land through their impassioned, loyal, and exasperated eyes.

It may be objected that many farmers, today, are not individuals or families: they are corporations, lacking personal attachment to the land they farm. Some of the lessons of Marin won't apply where the transition from farming to agribusiness is far advanced. But in fact the much-publicized death of the family farm in America is a long way from being fact. In most regions, farms, though growing in size, are still mostly family-owned; and this seems especially true in the metropolitan regions where farmland is under pressure from

When the founders of the Marin Agricultural Land Trust were doing their homework on how to deal in development rights, they had few models to look at. The most significant were three new state development-rights purchase programs in Maryland, Massachusetts, and Connecticut. There was also a cluster of local programs on the eastern end of Long Island, where governments were attempting to salvage some farmland from the eastward thrust of the New York metropolis.

Times have changed. Today there are nearly thirty efforts to purchase development rights going on, nationwide: seven conducted by states, fifteen by counties, four by cities and towns, and two by essentially private trusts (MALT is one of these; the second, the Solano County Farmland and Open Space Foundation, is just getting under way). In 1988, with the passage of Proposition 70, seven

Dolcini's Jersey cows

new county programs were launched in California alone.

Maryland's program is the oldest and, in gross terms, the most successful. The state has acquired rights on some seventy thousand acres. Massachusetts has secured over twenty-three thousand acres, Connecticut more than fifteen thousand. New Jersey and Vermont are coming on fast. Among the counties, the most notable are King County in Washington (the Seattle metropolitan region), with thirteen thousand acres, and Montgomery County in Maryland, where twenty thousand acres have been secured, mostly through a program for transfer of development rights.

The authors of later purchase programs have learned from the earlier ones. The newer programs tend to work faster and, in many cases, to pay somewhat more. To get more preservation for the buck, they may buy rights in carefully chosen areas, rather than haphazardly statewide or jurisdictionwide. They also tend to offer rights to purchase only where other measures, like strong zoning, are simultaneously being pursued. Combined with those other tools—the more of them, the better—such programs can even the odds, here and there, in the inherently unequal competition between development and traditional farm use.

urban growth. Policies like those adopted in Marin are likely, then, to support the family, not the large-scale corporate, variety of farm.

If we like what happened in West Marin, there follows a regret: that it happened on so small a scale. In the larger Bay Area, a campaign has been going on for years to do more widely what this one county has done narrowly: to set firm limits to horizontal growth, beyond which farms and other open lands remain—permanently. An organization called Greenbelt Alliance is pushing this plan in each county and talking up an eventual regionwide solution. Marin fits awkwardly into this movement, simply because it is ahead of the game: local conservationists, satisfied with things as they are, are reluctant to push for regional changes that might rock the local boat.

But when we remember the real scale of these problems—the issues of farmland loss and dissolving urban form—not even regional action looks all that significant. Only the states (or the federal government itself) have a reach wide enough to do much about them. Of the states that have gotten to work, one so far stands out. Oregon has for many years had a strong state planning law that requires cities to set definite boundaries to expansion, with farm and forest land beyond. (Oregon's defenses against parcel breakup on rural lands, the ranchette phenomenon, are, however, rather weak.) Florida, Georgia, and New Jersey have recently set up somewhat similar systems; Vermont has strengthened development controls already in existence. Hawaii, where limited land area forced early action, has had partially effective statewide zoning for years. Closer to home, California's coastal planning law is a model of large-scale land-use control, though confined to a narrow littoral strip. And a number of states along the great Atlantic urban corridor, from Maryland to Vermont, are now buying farmland development rights. The 1990s look like a big decade for such statewide programs.

What can local government do in and for this national movement? Above all, it can come up with a few good models. That has always been one of the arguments for strong small-scale governance: that cities and counties serve as laboratories, trying out individual solutions to common problems. It is pleasant to see in Marin County one of the cases—so much rarer than they ought to be—in which this promise has been fulfilled.

The Rancher Goes to Washington: Ralph Grossi
(Novato and Rockville, Maryland)

When dairyman Ralph Grossi was a boy on the family ranch outside Novato, he had no reasonable expectation of coming back there as a man. In 1961, a property just down the road was developed. "When the C ranch went," he recalls, "we were told we'd be out of here by 1970."

There never was doubt in Grossi's mind, though, about what he wanted to do. He trained himself for agriculture. When he came home from college, the ranch was still there, and county policies were changing. That suited the young man just fine. Buying into the family partnership, he got to work.

Soon he was involved with the Farm Bureau. "You see a need for something to be done, and so you inch forward. And if you inch forward in a farm community, you immediately get pulled in farther." He became the first chairman of a new Land Use Committee and drew into it a group of ranchers who were open minded about the county's suddenly restrictive zoning: Wilfred LaFranchi, Jim and Charles Spaletta, and Al Poncia, recently retired as Farm Bureau president. "We stuck our necks out pretty far sometimes," he says.

"A lot of the new leaders were sons of the old ones. They made it clear that they wanted to stay and make a life of it. That helped the farm community get used to the idea of A-60 zoning."

As the 1970s went on, Grossi became more and more an advocate for agriculture. His youth, his education, his speaking ability—even the location of his ranch, so near the urban fringe—made him visible. In 1979 he became Farm Bureau president, and shortly thereafter a founding director of MALT.

Meanwhile, back at the ranch, the same energy was showing. In 1980 he put the ranch on the map by installing a manure digester, the first in the

western United States. This vaguely boilerlike installation swallows manure and barn washings and "digests" them with the help of anaerobic bacteria into an odorless solid, an odorless liquid, and methane gas. (Making it do these things as advertised took several years.) The solid can be used for bedding material in dairies or as fertilizer (on test plots it has proved more effective than undigested manure). The liquid also has promise as a fertilizer, and the protein it contains might even be incorporated into a feed supplement. The methane can be burned to make electricity, enough for ranch needs and enough extra to sell to PG&E.

It was this electrical byproduct that got most of the press, but Grossi soon concluded it was secondary. If he had to do it again, he'd leave the generator out. "The damn thing accounted for half the cost of building and 80 percent of the maintenance costs." He recommends building digesters so that generators can be added later if energy prices warrant.

Ralph Grossi (right) and his father, Jim, branding cows. "Marin County is not an anomaly. It's very much a typical case of the problems farmers face everywhere on the urban fringe."

In 1986 came a surprising summons. The American Farmland Trust, the one nationwide organization devoted specifically to farmland preservation problems, tapped Grossi to be its new president. After weeks of indecision and long talks with his family, he went. "If I didn't take this," he explained, "I'd be milking cows at 3 A.M. some morning ten years from now, kicking myself for letting it go by." Eventually he sold his dairy allotment and converted his ranch to a beef operation that could be managed, more or less, by long-distance phone calls with his father.

In his new work, Grossi's farm background was an asset. "In fact, it was essential. I have had instant credibility with some groups because I have calluses on my hands." He glances at them. "*Had* calluses on my hands."

In the strange new world of Washington, Grossi's perspectives altered. Quickly he came to see how little the problem of saving farmland could be disentangled from the other problems facing American agriculture: contradictory government policies at all levels, mixed-up incentives that discourage farmers from planting new or different crops, lobbies that ignorantly work against their own long-term best interests.

No farm group, he notes ruefully, gives more money to its political action committees than does the dairy industry. "That works to our *dis*advantage." Dairy subsidies as now constituted, he is convinced, are doing the industry great harm.

"If we can't sell the product in the marketplace, our cooperative creamery picks up the phone, calls Uncle Sam, says 'I've got a truckload of powder or butter for you, come pick it up. If you can't pick it up, I'll store it here and you can pay me to store it.' That's how it works. . . . We now have processing plants that produce solely for the government." (The California Cooperative Creamery in Petaluma, it should be noted, is very far from being one of them.)

"The co-ops are supposed to pass the government money back to the dairies. But they actually keep much of it, sinking it into improvements to expand production. Then they turn around and tell us they need more milk to run the new facilities at maximum efficiency so they can sell more to the federal government." He laughs. "It's a vicious circle."

Grossi doesn't want the federal purchase program stopped outright. But he would like to see it strictly limited, say, to a set percentage of what is produced, creamery by creamery. Creameries would be obligated to buy some product back when the flow of milk is slack. The program would then serve to even out peaks and valleys in production—the original, long-lost idea.

Farmland, to Ralph Grossi, is much more than a platform to grow food on. It is inevitably also landscape, habitat, open space, a large and important part of the environment. If managed well, it serves several needs at once, lasts essentially forever, and demands little attention from anyone but its owners and managers. If there are to be subsidies, the trick is to organize them so that good practices, and not destructive ones, are encouraged. The 1985 farm bill took some steps in this direction by ending rewards for the plowing of virgin ground or of wetlands.

Issues like these get chewed on at the Washington headquarters of the American Farmland Trust, where leaders from environmental and agricultural groups meet regularly to shape legislation. In the 1985 farm bill debate, it was this small creative organization—staff of twenty—that pulled together the winning coalition. They are hoping to do it again.

How does the Marin experience fit into all this? "There is still some perception that Marin is an anomaly," Grossi notes. "Not so. It's very much a typical case of the problems farmers face everywhere on the urban fringe. And the solutions Marin worked out have meaning elsewhere." Among other things, the story shows how much can be done when a few key people get together. "And it shows you can make good progress if you're honest with people and lay everything on the table."

How long will Ralph Grossi stay in Washington? He plans to come back to the ranch on Novato Boulevard, where all the old dairy equipment is maintained against his return, in 1990 or 1991. But he's also waiting for a natural pause in the action. "If we're making progress, I guess I'd like to be part of the finish of what we're working on then. And if we don't make any . . . I'd be coming back under a sense of frustration . . . the wrong circumstances."

When Ralph Grossi comes back to Novato Boulevard, in other words, expect him to come back a winner.

Meanwhile, "it revitalizes me to visit once in a while and get on a tractor and push some manure around."

Border Station: The Strauses (Marshall)

When Ellen Prins told her New York friends that she was going west to marry a California dairyman, "they found it very strange. That was in 1950, and just at that time there was a big movement from the farm to the city. Everything was convenience. It was the beginning of frozen food, all that kind of thing . . . they thought that farms were all very backward.

"But this farm," she adds proudly, "was never backward."

"This farm," Ellen and William Straus's dairy ranch at Blake's Landing near Marshall, indeed has had its share of innovations. It was the first operation in West Marin to put in a stock-watering pond. It was the first to adopt the European practice of spreading barn washings on the fields. And over the years the fine irregular old farmhouse under the cypresses has served as a border crossing: a place where urban folk come to taste the realities of rural life, its charms and its endless labors.

The visits started informally late in the 1960s and multiplied in the early 1970s, when Drake and Redwood high schools began sending organized student groups. Besides brief tours, there were overnight camps and barbecues, and many youngsters returned to the ranch for summer work. The results were sometimes comical. "One year," Ellen recalls, "we had them paint the barn. One boy painted his name on the roof in huge red letters." But at least some students came away with an understanding, a grasp of the ranching world, that they would never lose. In later years, the visitors were more sedate groups from the Environmental Forum of Marin.

If the Strauses found it easy to talk to urbanites, it was partly because they had been city kids themselves: he raised in Hamburg, Germany; she in Amsterdam. But, partly for the same reason, they did not fit in so easily with their rural colleagues. In a region where most farm families were of Swiss-Italian or Portuguese extraction, now thoroughly Americanized, the Strauses were Jews, foreign-born, with slight but unshakable accents. In the solidly

Bill and Ellen Straus on their front porch in Marshall.
"Not too close and not too far from civilization."

Republican or apolitical farm belt, they were Democratic party activists.
And, most of all, in a region where such viewpoints were still strange and a
little scary, the Strauses were committed conservationists.

Even as they helped to educate urban folk about the realities of farm life,
they were taking stands that magnified their distance from their farm
compatriots.

Alone among the ranchers, the Strauses publicly supported Point Reyes
National Seashore.

Alone they opposed the high-density version of the West Marin General
Plan, which, among other things, called for a freeway past their front door and
a four-lane "parkway" riding the ridge in back.

Almost alone they testified in favor of A-60 zoning—and once saw the
hearing room empty as other ranchers walked out to protest their stand.

The Straus home in Marshall, built in 1864 by the New Hampshire pioneer Jeremiah Blake

Again and again they found themselves speaking against the religion of property rights—*I can do whatever I want to with my land.* "It always made you feel like you were unpatriotic," Bill recalls, "when you didn't agree with that."

Their eldest youngster, Albert, in high school at Tomales in those years, started an Ecology Club and gave his life savings—several pounds of coins in a Mason jar—to Gary Giacomini's first supervisoral campaign.

For a long time the cause seemed hopeless. Then, quite abruptly, county policies shifted in the direction the Strauses sought. And after that, much more gradually—too gradually to put firm dates on—the barriers between the Strauses and their fellow ranchers, built up high and hard in their years of opposition to community consensus, began to soften and come down.

The change goes back, perhaps, to the 1973 water pollution crisis, when Harold Gregg of the Marin Conservation League made Bill the league's representative on a Dairy Waste Committee formed by the Farm Bureau. "We simply got to know each other," says Bill. Other ranchers began to see that these strange environmentalist-farmers were farmers first of all and that, moreover, they were taking messages both ways. If they represented a preservationist viewpoint in the farm belt, they were also lecturing urban "ecologists"—underinformed and sometimes pretty self-righteous—about the farmers' needs.

Toward the end of the 1970s one young dairyman was heard to acknowledge out loud that the Strauses had been right to support A-60 zoning. Then came the movement for the Marin Agricultural Land Trust, based on an idea that Ellen had been pondering for years (it was Phyllis Faber, walking beside her in a spring-lush pasture after a farm tour, who said, "Let's do it"). Ellen has served on the MALT board from the beginning.

The day that an old antagonist, one of the most traditional of ranchers, came toward him on a street in Point Reyes Station with an extended hand and a smile, Bill knew that the gap had closed.

It was on a trip to Israel that Albert Straus first saw dairymen milking their animals three times a day. Back home, he tried it. The cows didn't drink much more or eat much more, but they did produce about 15 percent more milk.

Albert Straus examining his silage crop

That's the kind of experiment that Albert has pursued since he took over management of the family's Blake's Landing farms in 1977.

He's spent a lot of his time in those years struggling with one problem, a big problem, every dairy owner's biggest: the high cost of feed. Surely, he figured, there must be substances around, cheaper than the standard fare, that hadn't been tried on cows. He tried them. Lettuce trimmings and cabbage waste. Orange pulp and lima beans. Cocoa bean hulls ("with really strange results") and water hyacinth. Avocados. Wine lees. Tofu waste. Of all these various more-or-less-edibles, only one is currently in the ration: sake waste, the pressings that remain after manufacture of the Japanese-style rice wine.

Not that the sake experiment went all that smoothly, at first. Left to themselves, the cows would eat too much of the stuff. And once or twice they got drunk.

Passover seder at the Straus ranch

What does a drunk cow act like? "Same as you; wobbly. Falls over. . . . The milk tastes like sake for a while. And the hangover lasts about twenty-four to thirty-six hours." It's not as funny as it sounds. A drunk cow will roll over on its back, and a cow that lies upside down for any length of time can die. "I spent most of one night turning cows over. You grab their legs and roll 'em over. That's one experience I don't want to relive."

Like many ranchers these days, the Strauses are growing their own crops for silage. "It's coming around again to where that makes sense," Albert says. But here too he does things a little differently, using a "no-till" planting method in which the seeds are simply thrust into unturned soil. No-till saves time and labor; it also prevents erosion. "We get pretty close to the same tonnage on the land we till and the land we don't." At any one time, half the Straus fields are not tilled; the other half get very light tilling to incorporate manure (much better fertilizer than commercial chemicals). "It all goes back on the land."

When Albert Straus talks of the ranch, he is diffident, precise, all business. His deep feeling for this countryside—feeling he once tried to express in painting and in film—shows seldom in his conversation. But as a youngster, back in A-60 days, he wrote these words:

"Has anyone ever actually looked at Tomales Bay? The cattle and sheep graze over the land. The seals peer at you from the water. The hawks are sitting in the eucalyptus trees in groups of twenty. And then they take flight overhead. And then there is the blue heron, on a rock looking over the water.

"Some people are interested in saving the world. I'd like to save the world, too, but I don't know how, and perhaps for me it is better to start at home, where I love it."

The Clock that Moos: The Town of Point Reyes Station

In Point Reyes Station, informal capital of the West Marin dairy belt, they have a clock that moos. Twice a day, at noon and again at six, from the facade of the Old Western Saloon, the cow voice issues. It is amplified. It is in stereo. It can be heard, when the wind is right, for half a mile. Cows from the Waldo Giacomini dairy farm—its irrigated pastures showing green through the last row of houses—are likely to low back.

The Point Reyes Business Association conceived the project as a memorial to local historian Jack Mason. Sound engineers from Lucasfilm, Inc.—headquartered now on a ranch at Nicasio—supervised it, listening to tapes of several dozen cows to find the one that had the grandest, the most bovine, the most pungent moo.

The hick and the high tech, the self-consciously cute and the unsentimentally rural: Point Reyes Station—population three hundred fifty—is full of such mixtures. It's the kind of place, one visitor notes, "where businesses are still called by their owners' first names: Mike's Cafe, Ed's Superette, Toby's Feed Barn." But the local newspaper (housed in a former creamery) has won a Pulitzer. Feed store and art gallery, coffee shop and French restaurant, country

Western Weekend in Point Reyes Station

doctor and therapeutic massage: the place manages at once to be thoroughly rural and very much connected to the metropolitan area "over the hill."

Goulash? Mosaic? The whole West Marin countryside is like that. There are absolute wildlife sanctuaries; parks with classified wilderness areas in them; mountain lions sighted on the edge of little towns. There are movie production studios invisible in canyons. Religious retreats of several non-Western persuasions. A Christmas crèche with living donkey, sheep, and camel. Commuters to jobs "over the hill." Tourists by the million, and clogged weekend roads. People watching birds and people watching whales. Retired University of California professors (the links between Inverness and Berkeley are strong). Spanish-speaking laborers. An aging 1960s counterculture element. Artists of all sorts and qualities. Celebrations and informal holidays from Portugal, Switzerland, Mexico, Italy, and Spain. The Western Weekend and the livestock show . . .

Reading the daily police reports, which wind up now and then in the *New Yorker*'s "Constabulary Notes from All Over," you seem to be jerked from the 1960s to the 1990s, from the country to the city, from New Age troubles to the dusty indiscretions of the Good Old Boys. To someone used to more homogenous landscapes, the effect must seem scrambled.

But always—the fabric, still taken for granted—there are the ranches and the ranchers and the cows. This world could have a worse emblem than a clock that moos.

There is more than one reason for all this diversity. But what we're seeing here, most fundamentally, is a place that has done the heretofore almost impossible: it has imported city tastes and values without abandoning the country ones.

This countryside—even as it milks its cows, herds its sheep, nets its herring—has become a prototype of something very new in America: a *metropolitan* countryside, there by design, and very much attached to the urban world that, improbably enough, has become the guarantor of its survival.

Most rural places near cities are rural only because the city hasn't gotten to them yet. They are raw land. Temporary. Waiting. West Marin is no longer waiting. People here accept (though some fingers are still crossed) that the future will be as uncrowded as the past.

The *Point Reyes Light* remarked in 1977: "Battles that rage in other California communities—whether land-use planning is valid, whether anyone other than the landowner has a right to decide what environmental changes are tolerable—have been resolved here. Planning and conservation are givens in West Marin."

And the editorial pointed out one consequence: "The result has been more analysis in determining stands and less knee-jerk response to controversies. We certainly don't have any fewer disputes in West Marin than elsewhere. But at least debates here amount to more than drawing up the same battlelines over and over again regardless of the particular issue."

Mixture, again. Unexpected alliances—like the one that has been defending the agricultural inheritance. Unexpected divergences—like the split between those environmentalists who are more and those who are less solicitous of the farms' well-being.

Point Reyes Station, California: a sample of the possibilities, odd and fresh, that may emerge where the old colonial war of city on countryside is ended and replaced with something analogous to a negotiated peace.

Jersey cow

Appendix A ▪ A GRASSLAND HISTORY

Out in the countryside, where farmland is still farmland, the story runs back unbroken. In West Marin, old sites can be located, old names recognized in their old meanings. Old handhewn timbers can be spotted in working barns.

Take the Tomales Bay shoreline village of Marshall, for instance: named for the Marshall brothers, who in 1853 drove sixty head of pure-blood Durham cattle across the country from Kentucky. A descendant owns the original Marshall home ranch nearby.

Or take the traditional one-room rural school. California today has seven of these where kids still study. Three of them—Union, Lincoln, Laguna—are in Marin; ranch families have attended them for generations.

This stubbornly continuing story began as it goes on: with grass. Northwestern Marin and the adjoining part of Sonoma County make up California's largest single block of northern coastal prairie. When whites' settlement of the region began, the grassland consisted of perennial grasses, highly nutritious, green the year around. Over this superb range moved great herds of native tule elk and, as colonization progressed, still vaster herds of Mexican longhorn cattle.

In the 1820s, the county was essentially one vast cattle ranch attached to the Mission San Rafael Arcangel. The animals were valued not for milk or even meat but for their hides and tallow. For the most part they ran wild. Periodically the Mexican and Miwok Indian vaqueros rounded them up and drove them to the slaughterhouse at San Rafael; most of the flesh was discarded. (A traveler had the recognized right to kill another man's beast for food, if only he spared the hide.)

In 1834, the mission was shut down. The Mexican authorities began passing out the county to old soldiers and other applicants in vast, ill-defined swathes. The Miwoks, who were supposed to get a huge grant of their own, wound up landless as workers and squatters on the new ranchos. The owners (many of them Americans with Mexican citizenship) inherited the longhorn trade and its customers: other Yankees coming past in ships like the one Richard Henry Dana describes in *Two Years before the Mast.*

Came the Gold Rush, and beef was suddenly precious. Thousands of Marin longhorns were driven up to the gold country. Men made brief fortunes. But as the gold played out, the wild cattle lost their last value.

A more durable business began, the story goes, when local rancher Clara Steele had Miwok cowboys round up some longhorn cows, tie their hind legs together, and milk them. She made the county's first cheese. By the mid-1850s, dairying was well established, and a campaign was on to replace the feral Mexican cattle with more manageable American stock. The other competitor for the range—the tule elk—was already gone, wiped out locally, and very nearly as a species, by hunting and loss of habitat.

During all this early time another shift was going on. The green perennial grasslands were fading at last. With the first European contact had come seeds from the Old World, including numerous annual grasses and herbs from the Mediterranean region. These species, dying in summer but sprouting from seed each rainy season, are better able than perennials to withstand excessive grazing; over the decades, they had gradually been gaining ground.

In the early 1860s there was drought in California. The huge herds cropped their pastures to the root and found no more to crop. Statewide, it is estimated, three hundred thousand cattle died. And in Marin as elsewhere, the drought of 1862–1864 may have greatly accelerated the invasion of the annual grasses. From that time, perhaps, we can date the summer-yellow hills, the sudden vivid greens of winter, that we think of as typically Californian today.

Hard times brought by the drought also did much to break up the great old ranchos. As late as 1862 traveler William Brewer was complaining that two dozen families owned virtually all of Marin; ten years later most of the big blocks were shattered, and those that were intact were leased out to tenant dairy ranchers in units of a couple of hundred to a couple of thousand acres—just about the sizes that prevail today.

This tenant system was best developed on the cool grasslands of Point Reyes. Though the whole point had just two or three owners, it was rented to selected occupants in some thirty ranches, many named with letters of the alphabet. Tenants got not only land but also houses, barns, the cows themselves, and the most advanced equipment of the day. Climate, long grass, and expert management soon made the point the center of the dairy trade—"probably the greatest dairying section on the Pacific Coast," historian J. P. Munro-Fraser said.

The main dairy product of the 1860s and 1870s was not whole milk (which couldn't yet be shipped without spoilage) but butter. Put up in two-pound blocks and stamped with the prestigious label "P.R.," it sold for as much as a dollar a pound—at a time when a dollar might be a full day's wage. The second staple was cheese; the whey left over from its manufacture fed hogs. Shipped live to the city, these were the third main product.

There were few roads in the early days and no good ones, so the trade went by water. Almost every navigable cove had its wharf; steam-powered schooners came into Bolinas, to Drake's Estero on Point Reyes, and to various points on the shores of Tomales Bay. Shallow-draft lighters came in as far as the future site of Point Reyes Station (landlocked today).

Soon roads were getting better, and local money was building a rather improbable railroad. The Marin County timber industry, having nearly finished off the old-growth redwood forests of these hills, wanted rail access to the stands along the Russian River. The obvious route was up the eastern edge of the county and through Petaluma; but in those days the wealth and power in Marin lay west, not east, of the central divide. The railroad was brought "over the hill" from Fairfax, down the San Geronimo Valley and Papermill Creek, and north along the eastern shore of Tomales Bay. When service began in 1875, one unhappy rider compared the treeless Tomales shore to the desolation of the Arctic. James McMillan Shafter, one of the owners of Point Reyes, was frank about it: "There is a better place to build a railroad, but it don't lead to Olema or Tomales and that is the reason it is here."

The North Pacific Coast Railroad ran until the Russian River redwoods gave out, shutting down finally in 1933. Dikes, cuts, and fills mark its old course along the bay. On one ranch near Fallon, some of the old cuts, dammed at either end, make fine stock-watering ponds.

The towns of West Marin appeared in distinct batches. The first set—Bolinas, Olema, Nicasio, Lagunitas, Marshall, Tomales, San Geronimo—were natural crossroads or else lumbering centers; they got going in the 1850s. In the 1870s, when the railroad came, it skipped several of these older villages and produced several new ones, most notably Point Reyes Station and Fallon. After 1885 appeared a third layer of settlements, these developed for the tourist and second-home market: Muir Beach, Stinson Beach, Inverness, Inverness Park, Dillon Beach, Woodacre, Forest Knolls. Bolinas, once a booming lumber town, came back as a resort. Other centers have faded: historic Olema is a cluster of buildings surrounded by federal parkland; Fallon, where one big building used to house creamery, post office, tavern, and general store, is virtually gone; Dogtown, a raucous mill town once, is only a place-name.

The inhabitants came in batches, too. In the 1850s and 1860s, new arrivals in West Marin were likely to be Irish farmers leaving hunger behind at home. (Tomales was originally Keys Town for Irishman John Keys.) Ten years later, the typical immigrant was an Italian-speaking Swiss; one small region—the valley of the Maggia River in canton Ticino—was the source of most of Marin's Italian-surnamed families. Portuguese speakers were coming by then, too, in a long migration that peaked near the turn of the century; most came not from the European mainland but from the Azores (in some cases by way of Hawaii). Just after World War I another sizable contingent arrived from the coast of Yugoslavia, from the offshore islands of Iz and Hvar: these people—their names often ending in -*ich*—tended to take up fishing in the new country as in the old.

And there was to be a fifth wave: this one from the district of Jalisco near Guadalajara in Mexico. Though the source is closer this time, the pattern seems the same. Men arrive first and go to work on the ranches. In a few years, they have enough money set aside to bring families after them. One difference is that, in these times of high land prices, it is more difficult for the new arrivals to work up to owning ranches; most eventually go back to the homeland.

Water tower in Tomales

Of the several hundred ranches in the Marin-Sonoma dairy belt, only a few have Spanish-surnamed owners.

All the while, the dairy industry was changing. At first, butter- and cheese-making happened on every ranch. But soon, as liquid milk became a transportable product requiring pasteurization, creameries opened in Point Reyes Station, Fallon, and elsewhere. These consolidated over the decades until, today, the California Cooperative Creamery in Petaluma serves the entire region and processes 85 percent of its milk. (Safeway is the other major buyer.) Herd size meanwhile grew beyond what local fields could sustain, and farmers began buying feed from the Central Valley. Recently, though, higher prices have led more and more farmers to start growing hay again.

There was a time when most farms in West Marin were dairies. Today there is actually more land in sheep and cattle ranches, producing meat and wool, as well as replacement heifers for the dairy herds. It's proverbially hard to make a living on sheep and cattle alone, without taking other work on the side, but some operators are trying. Several ranches are producing a new type of premium beef, lean and raised without the heavy use of antibiotics that is typical in the modern meat industry; the product sells well in the health-conscious East Marin market. Poultry, important in the past, has dwindled, but the huge Nicholas Turkey Breeding Farm near Tomales is part of a two-county operation that supplies half the worldwide demand for turkey eggs for hatching, and the "Willie Birds" of turkey grower William Benedetti are regionally famous.

Nobody who's seen what a backyard garden will grow in West Marin will be surprised that vegetables, too, have been big business here. Greater or lesser acreages have been planted to beets, grains, and—above all—to potatoes. The potato boom, lasting from the 1850s to about 1900 and centered at Tomales, marked the land forever. The steep local hillsides could not take the cultivation. The resulting erosion stripped the fragile soil, lowered the land surface by a foot or more on many thousands of acres, and sent millions of tons of sediment into Tomales Bay. It also, of course, ended the industry that caused it. When the light is right, you can see the old plow marks up and down the hills.

Other crops have been less damaging. Before World War II, Japanese and Italian farmers grew asparagus, peas, and artichokes on flatter parts of Point Reyes. Even today truck gardens do well in sheltered spots; gourmet mushrooms are growing in several ranch basements; and one vintner is confident that West Marin climate and soils would be ideal for certain grapes.

People concerned for this landscape like such talk. They watch with approval every sign of diversity, of new products flowing from the land. The more varied the agriculture, they reason, the stabler; the less vulnerable to economic shocks; the more able to resist the always-present pressure to subdivide.

But for the time being, at least, the dairy and livestock industries in Marin overshadow all the rest. The land remains as it began, a place of grass.

Spaletta ranch

Appendix B ▪ W H A T   M A R I N   C O U N T Y
D I D (and Didn't Do)

Of the many tools that Marin County has used in its campaign to keep agriculture and agricultural land intact, not one is, strictly speaking, unique.

On the other hand, if we list the various tools that local governments (or local voters!) might use to preserve farmland, it appears that this county has missed hardly a bet.

Such a list—based on examples nationwide—might look something like this:

Define sharply the area to be preserved. (In Marin, topography eased this job; the three-corridor concept in the Marin Countywide Plan made expectations clear.)

Protect that area from new highways and other public works projects that would favor urban development. (Citizens' opposition in Marin killed several proposed freeway projects well before other pro-farmland policies came along; the countywide plan made it official policy to keep such infrastructure out of the rural zone.)

Zone the area to prevent widespread development at urban densities—or, better, to prevent non-farming development at all. (Marin's A-60, though hardly drastic, has served the purpose—so far.)

Purchase parks and open-space lands along the urban-rural edge. Or use easements to strip the development potential from lands in the buffer zone. (In Marin, nearly all the urban-rural boundary has now been sealed with government-owned land.)

Tax farmland gently, according to the farm income it produces rather than according to a market value influenced by the possibility of development. (California's 1965 Agricultural Land Conservation Act, known as the Williamson Act, was one of the earliest such measures; Marin County was the first in California to conclude a Williamson Act contract with a rancher.) A variation on the same idea: avoid taxing farmland for the support of essentially urban services that farmers seldom use.

Protect farm operations with "right-to-farm" laws. These serve notice to people who settle in farm areas that farming has priority, and that complaints about ordinary smells and noises of agriculture, for example, will not be entertained. (Marin has no policy in this direction, though an informal understanding seems to prevail.)

Keep the urban public and political leaders interested in the nature, values, and problems of local agriculture. (Marin has its Family Farm Days, the work of the Environmental Forum, and educational work by the Farm Bureau in the schools.)

Set up marketing efforts to help local farmers sell their produce at good prices. In particular, make it easy for local people to find and buy fresh local products. (Marin has several farmers' markets, and some beef, vegetable, and shellfish raisers have connections to local stores. Most local milk, however, disappears into a regional pool.)

Be ready to subsidize farmers in times of crisis. (Marin did this dramatically with its drought and pollution control aid.)

Speak up on behalf of farm viewpoints whenever common interests permit. (No other kind of support impressed Marin ranchers quite so much as the backing of local conservationists and the county government in the 1977 milk-price hearings.)

Set up a program to purchase development "rights," transfer them to more suitable areas, or both. The body that does this may also give support of other kinds. (Marin has, of course, the Agricultural Land Trust and county rights-transfer ordinances.)

There are also notable things that Marin County did not do.

Greatly though it succeeded in protecting farmland and rural open space, the county did much less well on other goals of its countywide plan. It did not succeed, for instance, in setting up the comprehensive transit service it called for, or in drawing many people away from almost sole reliance on the private car as the way of getting around. It has not succeeded well in providing housing for people of low, or even of moderate, incomes. (Few of the longtime residents of Marin cities could afford to buy the houses they now occupy, if they were starting out again.) The county and its cities may have succeeded all too well in another goal of the plan: to add to local industry and jobs. Employment has expanded much faster than housing, making Marin a commuter target for people from Sonoma County and further clogging the roads.

All in all, the county has not fulfilled the other half of the program announced in the countywide plan: to develop, as counterpart to the rural zone out west, an eastern corridor that was to be richly, efficiently, and, in parts rather densely, urban.

To say the least, Marin is not alone in its failures. Hardly a part of the state or the nation has really succeeded in handling large-scale problems like these. It is a question whether local government, as now constituted, is capable of handling them. (Even Marin's Countywide Plan never lived up to its hopeful name: those incorporated cities where growth was vigorous, where basic land-use decisions remained to be made, have paid little attention to it.) And who is equipped to answer the basic question, the awesome question, the one ignored in the typical local battle over "growth": where should they live, the people being added daily to the population?

One thing, though, is clear: Had the county failed to hold the line in West Marin—had it let its agriculture go—neither county nor region would be better off in any respect. The Bay Area would have gained only another ring of diffuse, expensive, auto-dependent suburbia. Housing would not be cheaper. Traffic would not flow more smoothly. The ranches would, by now, be gone or going. So would the Tomales Bay shellfish farms. And where would be the gain?

That Marin County failed, as it dealt with one basic problem, to solve various others: this hardly detracts. (How often do governments solve even one?) As it is, this community managed to carry out a piece of fundamental research whose eventual applications can be, ought to be, wide.

We thank the following people who gave generously of their time to allow us glimpses into their lives. They are part of the strength and fabric that make up West Marin.

Fred Bauer	*Rancher, llamas*
Peter Behr	*Former state senator*
Kathleen and Willie Benedetti	*Ranchers, goat and turkey*
Anne Burbank and Georgia Marino	*Tomales historians; ranchers, beef*
Cory and Jerry Corda	*Ranchers, dairy*
Mary Dolan and Martin Strain	*Oyster growers*
Betty Dolcini	*Rancher, beef and horses*
Earl and Micky Dolcini	*Ranchers, dairy and beef*
Sharon Doughty	*Rancher, dairy*
Agnes and Leroy Erickson	*Ranchers, sheep, beef, and dairy replacement heifers*
Phyllis Faber	*Biologist*
Jerry Friedman	*Marin County Planning Commissioner*
Alvin and Doris Gambonini	*Ranchers, beef*
Gary Giacomini	*Supervisor, District 4, Marin County*
Robert Giacomini	*Rancher, dairy*
Annette and George Grossi	*Ranchers, dairy and beef*
Ralph Grossi	*President, American Farmland Trust*
Tim Hollibaugh	*Oyster grower, marine biologist*
Anna Jensen	*Rancher, sheep and beef*
Jean and Skip Kehoe	*Ranchers, dairy*

Wilfred LaFranchi	*Rancher, dairy*
Joan and Joe Lunny	*Ranchers, beef*
Harold P. Maloney, M.D.	*Gericke family historian*
Bob, Jim, and Ron McClure	*Ranchers, dairy*
Dorothy McClure	*McClure family historian*
Dorothy and Merv McDonald	*Ranchers, beef*
Denise and Neil McIsaac, Jr.	*Ranchers, dairy*
Joe and Linda Mendoza, Jr.	*Ranchers, dairy*
Bill Niman	*Organic beef producer*
Lois Parks	*Tomales historian; rancher, sheep*
Al and Cathie Poncia	*Ranchers, dairy*
Ed Pozzi	*Rancher, sheep and beef*
Otto Quast	*Plant propagator*
Nina and Philip Respini	*Ranchers, sheep*
David and Sharon Righetti	*Ranchers, dairy*
Wendy Johnson Rudnik	*Supervisor, Green Gulch Farm operations*
John Sansing	*Superintendent, Point Reyes National Seashore*
Russell Sartori	*Rancher, dairy*
John Siebert	*Economist, California Cooperative Creamery*
Frank and Millie Spenger, Jr.	*Restaurant owners and fishermen*
Boyd and JoAnn Stewart	*Ranchers, beef and horses*
Albert Straus	*Rancher, dairy*
Bill and Ellen Straus	*Ranchers, dairy*
Gordon Thorton	*Rancher, sheep, beef, and dairy*
John Vilicich	*Boat builder and fisherman*
Warren Weber	*Organic vegetable grower*
George Wheelwright	*Rancher, beef*
Andy Zorba	*Oyster grower*

Page numbers in italic indicate photographs

Designer: Steve Renick
Compositor: G&S Typesetters, Inc.
Text: 12/16 Garamond
Display: Garamond
Printer: U. C. Printing Services
Binder: U. C. Printing Services